PaulaPrykeLivingColour

Gold-green shot silk covers an egg-
shaped vase which coordinates
perfectly with the bright green centres
of Amazon lily (*Eucharis grandiflora*).
The shaggy chrysanthemum
(*Dendranthema* 'Revert') forms a collar
around the base of the lily stems.

A cobalt-blue moon vase is
filled with groups of
delphinium (*Delphinium
belladonna* 'Volkerfrieden'),
lime-green chrysanthemums
(*Dendranthema* 'Revert')
and the green anthurium
(*Anthurium* 'Midori')
to produce this
informal display.

PaulaPryke

Living Colour

PHOTOGRAPHY BY **DAVID LOFTUS**

jacqui
small

This book is dedicated to the memory of a very
special lady and gifted florist, Lynne Lawrence
(21 April 1948 – 20 July 1999).

A blade of grass

You ask for a poem.
I offer you a blade of grass.
You say it is not good enough.
You ask for a poem.

I say this blade of grass will do.
It has dressed itself in frost,
It is more immediate
Than any image of my making.

You say it is not a poem,
It is a blade of grass and grass
Is not quite good enough.
I offer you a blade of grass.

You are indignant.
You say it is too easy to offer grass.
It is absurd.
Anyone can offer a blade of grass.

You ask for a poem.
And so I write you a tragedy about
How a blade of grass
Becomes more and more difficult to offer,

And about how as you grow older
A blade of grass
Becomes more difficult to accept.

© BRIAN PATTEN 1981

Publisher Jacqui Small
Designer Robin Rout
Editor Bella Pringle
Production Geoff Barlow

First published in 2001
by Jacqui Small,
an imprint of Aurum Press Ltd,
7 Greenland Street,
London NW1 0ND

This paperback edition
published in 2008

ISBN 978-1-903221-77-8

Printed and bound in China

2008
10 9 8 7 6 5 4 3 2 1

CONTENTS

For a limited period in early summer, onion-shaped seedheads of allium are sold as cut flowers. Here, I have produced a structured display by arranging the alliums in two tiers. A single leaf of flax (*Phormium tenax*) is glued to the vase to accentuate the linear effect.

Impact of

Colour

In my life, the colour of flowers and plants has always been central, supporting me, enthralling me and inspiring me. From an early age, I was acutely aware of colour, intoxicated by the colours in nature and the impact they had on the environment.

I had a thoroughly rural upbringing and from an early age was fascinated by wild flowers and plants. I loved any activity that involved colour, I was addicted to the haberdashery departments of large stores and had a huge collection of embroidery threads.

At university, I dreamed about opening a small flower shop, and was the proud owner of an impressive indoor plant display, but really had no understanding of the retail side of floristry. The turning point came on Valentine's Day in 1985 when, driving across London, I saw bright red bouquets on every street corner and resolved to immerse myself in the flower industry. I enrolled on a part-time professional floristry course and, two years later, took the plunge and opened my first flower shop. By good fortune, my natural style of arranging was well received and my new business flourished. Twelve years on, my displays are still inspired by the colours found in nature and I still try to make flower colour the star of the arrangement rather than the design.

Colour is the most important element in any flower arrangement because it sets the mood of the display – the colours can be vibrant and arresting or calm and soothing. The technical skills involved in arranging flowers can be learned but I believe we are all born with our own personal response to colour. The way we 'see' colour can be very different from the next person and what one person may consider to be bright and colourful, another may consider garish. When I was young, I loved deciding which

clothes went well together and my girlfriends often sought my advice. I think these early lessons in colour mixing helped shape my understanding of how colours interact.

The best way to start your journey with flower colour is first to experiment with your own favourites and then move through the wider palette available to the florist. This way you will discover the colours and textures in different plant materials and accessories. My working relationship with flowers and foliage has made me aware of the wealth of natural colour available. When you examine the petals of an individual flower you discover that each one has its own unique colour palette. Even a single species of flower, grown in varying climates and soil types, can produce different results. For example, hydrangea petals turn pink in acid soil and blue in alkaline. Many plants, especially trees, change colour with the seasons. In spring, deciduous trees produce fresh lime-green new leaves, and when autumn comes, a radical colour change takes place from green to red, orange and brown – quickly transforming the landscape. The weather plays an important part in determining how dramatic and interesting the colours of autumn will be. A crisp cold autumn following a dry warm summer produces the best autumn blaze.

Here, burgundy *Rosa* 'Black Magic' are brought together with bright yellow *Rosa* 'Taxi', deep pink *Rosa* 'Milano' and lilac-blue *Rosa* 'Blue Curiosa'. This is an unusual colour mix but by using dark burgundy roses I have successfully harmonised bright pink, lilac and yellow.

Colour in nature

The colours of flowers and plants are intended for the animal kingdom and the message is simple – the flowers are attracting the attention of birds, animals and insects for pollination. The insects and birds are fed by the nectar and the flowers are rewarded by fertilisation. Although some plants can self-pollinate, most require cross-pollination, a process that creates a more genetically diverse plant kingdom. Bright-coloured flowers like hibiscus usually require birds to move from flower to flower to pollinate them. Plant species that produce red berries in autumn, like holly or mountain ash, aim to attract fruit-eating birds that will later excrete the undigested seeds, triggering new plant growth.

Colour symbolism

There has always been a close connection between natural plant colour and human activity. Natural colours extracted from minerals, plants, insects and animals were used by the wealthy in ancient civilisations in Egypt, the Roman Empire and the Islamic world for paintings and to dye textiles. This connection still manifests itself in everyday life in India, where colour plays an essential part in the Hindu religion. At weddings, brides are sprinkled with yellow turmeric, yellow clothes are worn and yellow food is eaten. At the festival of Holi, coloured powder and water is dispersed though the crowds. In the Christian world, colours have also had cultural and religious significance. Purple was associated with God, power and dignity. Red is the colour of love and Christmas but at the same time it is the colour of sacrifice. Used in combination, colours also take on meanings. For example, red and white are associated with blood and war and are the colours on the Red Cross flag.

Colour to create mood

Colour also has a powerful psychological impact and can influence our state of mind. Some colours are regarded as 'healing', making us feel happy and well, while others have a negative impact, inducing melancholy.

Many of these emotional responses to colour have become expressions in everyday speech. We refer to 'black' moods, to feeling 'blue' and 'seeing red'. When we hear about people or situations 'lacking colour' we presume that they are unwell or boring.

In the early nineteenth century the great German poet Goethe recognised the emotional power of colour and developed a colour theory which emphasised its previously neglected spiritual significance.

The use of flowers in the home illustrates the mood-enhancing powers of colour. A floral display is the simplest way of changing the atmosphere of an interior. The introduction of yellow flowers will create a bright and happy ambience, while white or green arrangements create a feeling of calm and serenity.

The colour wheel

In 1669, Isaac Newton proved that when light is dispersed, we see colour. All the colours of the spectrum are in daylight but we cannot see them with the naked eye except when a rainbow occurs. This amazing arc of colour is caused by the refraction and internal reflection of light in rain drops, which causes white light to break up into eight colours – red, orange, yellow, green, turquoise, blue, violet and magenta. Often these colours are presented schematically on a colour wheel to help us understand their precise relationship to one another in the colour spectrum.

Although a colour wheel is useful when working with nature, it is more complex for the flower arranger than for the artist using paints. In traditional displays, green foliage creates the background, structure and shape of the arrangement and the choice of foliage helps to set the tone of the display.

Colour control

It is difficult to maintain strict colour control in most floral arrangements, because most flowers have stamens or centres in different colours from the petals, green stems and leaves. There are too many other elements at play that will affect the colour combination. In the end, a good mix of colours depends on the shape and scale of the flowers as much as the petal colour, or the use of foliage. But the current fashion for tightly packed monochromatic arrangements – with foliage removed – allows for stricter colour control.

Here, hot pink, red and purple are mixed with lime green to produce an arresting display. These colours work together because they have equal colour saturation and intensity. The textured flowerheads of the red and pink celosia (*Celosia cristata* 'Bombay Pink' and 'Red Chief') create bold blocks of colour for maximum impact.

Hot and cool colours

The colour temperature of a display and our emotional response to it are key to the flower arranger. Hot colours like bright pink usually stand out and demand more attention than cooler shades like blue. On one side of the colour wheel we have all the warm-to-hot colours – including the warmer blues and purples. These follow on to red, with magenta pink in between. Then come orange and yellow. On the other side of the colour wheel are the cool complementary colours, shades of blue and green.

Colour tones

Every colour has a dark or light tone which influences its relation to other colours. White and black are the tonal extremes and although there are no truly black flower colours there are some very dark ones that produce a similar effect. Black flowers serve as a backdrop to bright flower colours and enhance their dramatic role in an arrangement. White flowers lighten displays and soften the end result.

A number of colourful red, pink and white zinnias have been used in concentric circles to create this dome-shaped display. It gives a modern feel to these traditional country garden flowers.

Identifying flower colours

On a more practical level, when you are looking for flower varieties in one particular colour, knowledge of the Latin species name may help. Often the species name is related to the flower colour so it acts as a useful key. '*Alba*', for example, is a well-known term for white and is a helpful classification. The number of different shades of red flower means that various terms have arisen. Blood-red flowers are often classified as '*sanguineum*'. *Geranium sanguineum*, therefore has bright red flowers, while '*coccinea*' promises scarlet flowers after the scarlet-coloured insect dye cochineal. '*Aurea*' indicates golden-coloured petals or leaves, while '*purpurea*' describes purple flowers like those of the foxglove *Digitalis purpurea*. Take care though, as sometimes the Latin name came be a little misleading. '*Niger*' for example, in *Helleborus niger*, can refer to the black root of the plant as well as to the flower.

Labelling flowers

Sometimes our efforts to use the correct flower name can be thwarted. Often, the growers do not label the flowers or the salespeople in markets and wholesale businesses do not supply the correct name on the invoice or box. This makes selecting flowers by colour quite difficult. When ordering flowers, try to use the variety name, and write down the colour you require. When I need an exact colour match, I provide a flower name as a reference. For instance, if I need a gerbera to match a gloriosa lily then I will ask my supplier for a 'gloriosa-pink gerbera'. Or, if I'm ordering celosia, which is available in many shades of red, I may specify a deep red like *Rosa* 'Grand Prix', as this is well-known to suppliers.

My business is only a few hours away from the flower auctions in the Netherlands where nearly seventy per cent of the world's flower supply originates. This gives me an exciting choice to select from and almost every week a new coloured variety becomes available.

Colour as the starting point

When I have total freedom of choice for a design, I always begin by taking one flower and use it as my guide. Sometimes it will dictate a monochromatic colour scheme or it may lead to a new colour combination. Usually, my first thought is what will work well with that colour. I love experimenting and trying out new colour mixes. I love deep colours like burgundy and purple set against hot oranges and pinks. For example, I use burgundy cotinus foliage (*Cotinus coggygria* f *purpurea*) with orange roses (*Rosa* 'Naranga') and leucospermums (*Leucospermum cordifolium* 'Coral'), or contrast purple alliums and lisianthus with hot pink bougainvillea. I also like to reconsider colour mixes that have faded in popularity with florists and try to reinvent them. For example, I enjoy the rich combination of deep pink and purple anemones with rosy peach roses like *Rosa* 'Femma', and I also enjoy experimenting with coral-pink flowers, such as peonies (*Paeonia* 'Coral Charm').

Blocks of colour

The flower market is the single most important place for my inspiration. Here I see flowers massed together in large quantities, which helps me to to see at first hand the effect one colour has on another and to visualise future combinations. For example, when yellow is placed next to red, it is amplified, while lime green with blue makes the blue appear brighter and more saturated. Vivid orange in association with dark burgundy makes the deep red appear a more confident colour. I also find that colour blocking flowers in my shop offers inspiration for flower colours that will work well together in a display as well as

making the shop look very attractive. For example, flower buckets of the pale rose 'Bianca Candy' next to peach amaryllis (*Hippeastrum* 'Rilona') may suddenly trigger an idea for a unusual salmon peach design.

Floral craft

Looking back on my career, I now see my contribution – and that of other talented young florists in London – in helping transform the public perception of floristry from a craft to an art form with a rich palette of colour. Cut flowers have now become a fashion statement. The heart of my business is still the shop but my floristry portfolio is now more diverse, including work for television and media events, floral contracts for offices, banks, hotels and restaurant reception areas and designing party and wedding flowers.

Here, pale pink *Rosa* 'Royal Renata' have been arranged with waxed apples to create a monochromatic table centrepiece. Fruit and vegetables often provide the colour inspiration for floral displays.

In 1994, I started to teach flower arranging to a keen band of enthusiasts from around the world, and now lectures and demonstrations and my flower school programme are fitted in around my other projects. When I spend time away from flowers, I always feel that same flush of excitement for their colours and scent when I return. There is a Japanese proverb which says 'Happiness is to hold flowers in both hands' I agree completely!

Inspired by nature

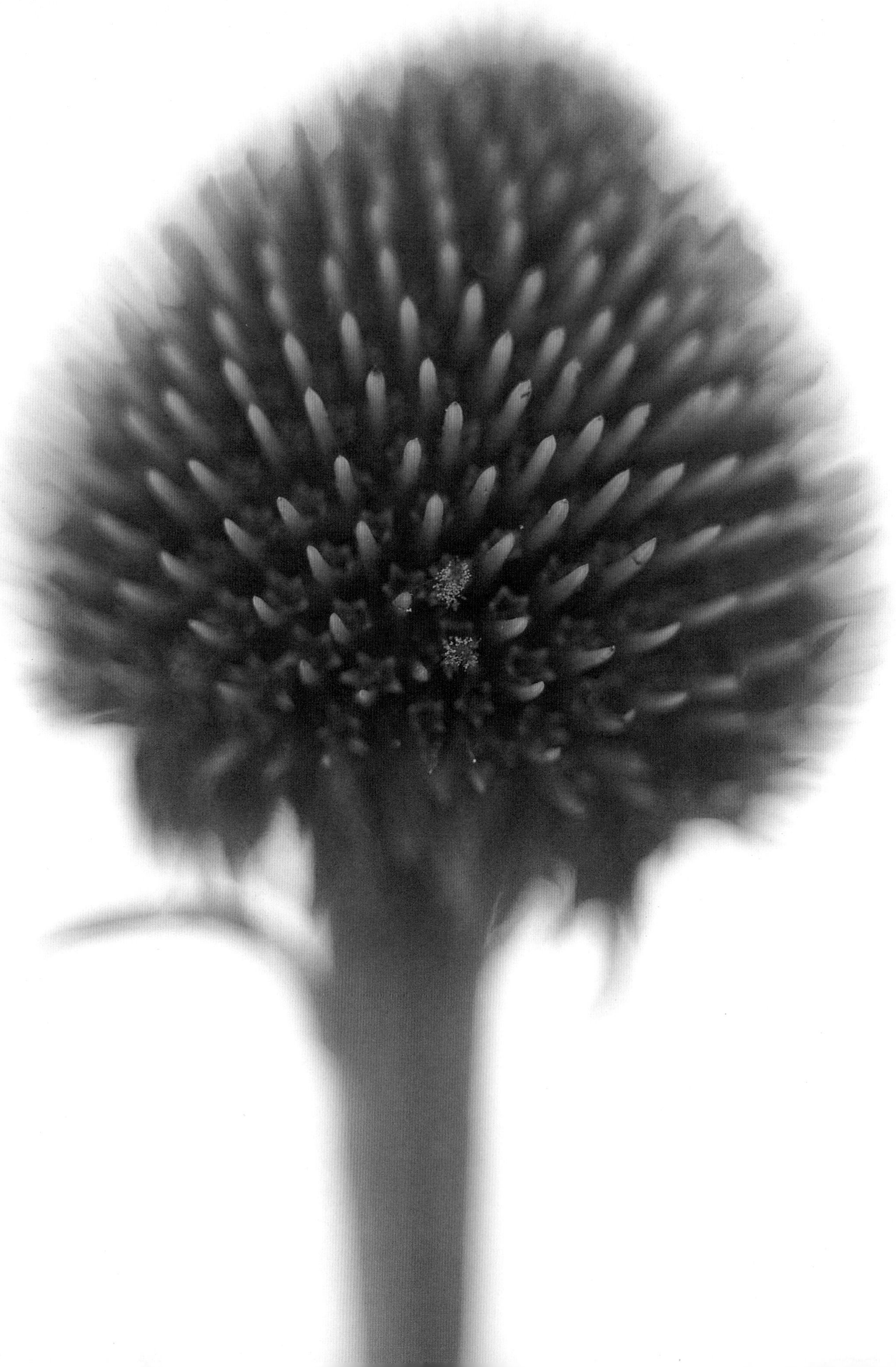

Be inspired and learn how to create stunning floral displays by observing how colours and patterns combine in the natural world. Take ideas for flower designs from studying the gradation of colour on petals, the markings on stems, the shift in leaf colour from one season to the next, and the texture and hues found in fruit, berries and bark. Let nature be your guide.

In my work, I often choose to follow the floral colour schemes I have seen in nature. Flowers have helped shape the way I view colour in the world and have taught me how to be more confident and experimental when bringing colours together. Nature is a very good teacher and the influence it has on all our lives should not be underestimated. Flowers mark every occasion and most of our rituals and nature is believed by many cultures to yield divine inspiration. In Japan, for example, I observed the custom of *hanami* or 'flower-viewing' which is part of the Japanese appreciation of the beauty of nature. *Hanami* is regarded as an important activity for refreshing the senses. Like the Japanese, I recognise that there is something spiritually healing about working with flower colour – beyond the simple pleasure they give us when growing in gardens or the wild.

Nature as teacher

Seasonal colour mixes inspire my floral palette. Blue and yellow combinations are stimulated by walks in the woods in spring, where the ground is carpeted with bluebells interspersed with yellow cowslips and marsh marigolds. In late summer, I am drawn to bright yellow and purple-pink colour combinations seen in hedgerows, where solidago and clumps of pink knapweed grow freely. At the end of the year – again following nature's lead – I indulge in a rich earthy palette of red, orange, yellow and brown flowers, foliage and berries, before winter sets in and the choice of colours in nature shifts to silvers and greys.

Often, inspiration for a floral scheme comes direct from one flower type. For example, a beautiful orange strelitzia with purple markings suggests an orange-purple mix with purple aconitum and liatris. Parrot tulips with their fiery red and yellow markings direct me to yellow blossom, such as forsythia, while the striped purple and white 'Rembrandt' tulip – which inspired the English interior designer David Hicks – suggests a mix with burgundy ranunculus and silver pussy willow. In *Inspired by Nature* some of my favourite colour combinations have arisen from one flower, such as the black-eye and yellow petals of the *Gerbera jamesonii* 'Esperanza' or the distinct markings on the lime-green cymbidium orchid. The chequer board markings of snake's head fritillary (*Fritillaria meleagris)* are equally inspiring, and suggest a regimented style display even though the flower is quite wild and natural. Interestingly, flowers and foliage from different climatic zones do not seem to work together harmoniously unless they are an exact match and have the same intensity of hue.

A delicate balance

The fragility and ephemeral nature of flower petals also informs my work. It is the fleeting beauty of flowers that makes them so special. My favourite moment is the point when the flower has passed perfection but is still in full bloom. For garden roses, it is the stage when the head is heavy and about to drop.

In my own work, I tend to prefer simple clean shapes for arrangements. I look to nature to understand how these forms grow, so that I can replicate them in my work. Heliconias, calla lilies, nerines, amaryllis and agapanthus all have long, leaf-free flower stems and display the simple architectural quality that I favour. I tend to arrange these flower types without foliage in an attempt to mirror their natural growth habit. Bare trees and stems are a source of inspiration for designs, as are many leaf and flower formations.

A truly great florist follows nature's design and uses it as a foundation for their floral work. 'Vegetative' and 'natural' styles are well established in traditional floristry, and aspiring flower arrangers are encouraged to capture the animation of nature in their designs. The famous Constance Spry flower school in the UK where I underwent my training described this natural quality as 'leaving room for the butterflies!'

Left Natural textures are as important in my work as colour. One of my favourite textures is given by flowering seedheads, like rudbeckia (*Rudbeckia hirta*), shown here in microscopic detail. The chocolate-brown rudbeckia seedheads are more prized by florists than the flowers in bloom and are gathered in summer when the lavender-pink petals have started to droop. Rudbeckia seedheads are now grown all around the world for use in cut-flower displays and are available throughout the year.

Gloriosa lilies are just sensational. I love the surprising juxtaposition of their fragile delicate forms set against clashing fuchsia pink and lemon-yellow colour.

TROPICAL COLOUR

Inspired by this fiery colour mix, I have used an equally intense palette of flowers, heightened by vivid lime and forest-green foliage.

In the tropics, the bright sunshine dictates vibrant colour combinations like that offered by *Gloriosa rothschildiana*, and pale-coloured flowers are simply bleached out by the sheer intensity of the sunlight. This stunning little flower, first discovered by Z.W. Baron de Rothschild whilst bird-watching in Africa, makes a powerful impact. The fuchsia-pink petals are edged in bright yellow, and so offer a rich colour palette to work with. Here, they provide the inspiration from nature for a tropical-coloured hand-tied bouquet. To make this vivid colour display even bolder, and also to introduce more textural interest, I like to mix it with lacy lime-green foliage, such as lady's mantle (*Alchemilla mollis*) or, as shown here, the spiky tendrils of acid-green chrysanthemum (*Dendranthema* 'Shamrock'). Then, to make the arrangement appear stronger and deeper in tone, rather than too lurid and violent, I always use some dark green foliage, in this instance the shiny forest-green leaves of *Ruscus aculeatus*. When working with hot pinks and yellows, the balance of colour throughout the display is key, and green foliage works to anchor the hotter colours visually.

This spectacular *Gloriosa* species is rare among bulb plants because it is a climber. The lily stems can grow to about 1.8m (6ft) high. *Gloriosa rothschildiana* is heavily cultivated in hothouses throughout the Netherlands and each fragile long stem is cut to length when exported.

DETAILS OF DISPLAY

PINK
2 *Celosia argentea* 'Cristata No 9'
6 *Gerbera jamesonii* 'Emperor'
12 *Gloriosa rothschildiana*
5 *Hypericum* 'Dolly Parton'

GREEN
3 *Anethum graveolens* 'Green Dille'
5 *Dendranthema* 'Shamrock' (Chrysanthemum)
5 *Ruscus aculeatus*

YELLOW
3 *Zantedeschia aethiopica* 'Florex Gold' (Calla lily)

Other flower choices

PINK	GREEN	YELLOW
Dahlia 'Pontiac'	*Alchemilla mollis* (Lady's mantle)	*Achillea filipendulina* 'Moonshine'
Gerbera jamesonii 'Magnum'	*Hypericum* 'Autumn Blaze'	*Centaurea macrocephala*
Rosa 'Daytona de Meilland'	*Dendranthema* 'Kermit' (Chrysanthemum)	*Craspedia globosa*
Rosa 'Jacaranda'	*Leucadendron* 'Safari Sunset'	*Helianthus annus* 'Sunrich Orange'
Rosa 'Ravel'		*Lysimachia vulgaris*
Rosa 'Renate Splendid'		*Rosa* 'Papillon'

DARK EYES

Bearing a remarkable resemblance to the way a child might draw a flower, gerberas are high on many people's favourite flower list. Their sunny disposition, bold arrangement of petals and dark eyes, appeal to our senses and form the foundation on which this strong yellow and black arrangement is based.

Originally from the sunny climate of the Transvaal in South Africa, these brightly coloured gerbera daisies bring sunshine and confidence to any style of arrangement. For the colourist, the gerbera is a remarkable flower. As a result of successful hybridisation, gerberas are now grown in vast quantities in an astonishing choice of shades and are available in single, double and shaggy forms. I am especially fond of the black-eyed varieties, such as *Gerbera jamesonii* 'Esperanza', used in this display, because of the dramatic contrast between the petal colour and the central black eye within each flowerhead. Here, I have grouped together gerberas (*Gerbera jamesonii* 'Esperanza') with yellow Afro-French marigolds (*Tagetes erecta* 'Promise Yellow'), yellow roses (*Rosa* 'Sphinx') and calla lilies (*Zantedeschia aethiopica* 'Florex Gold').These flowers are then contrasted with rudbeckia seedheads (*Rubdbeckia hirta)* and the glossy dark green leaves and black berries of fruiting ivy (*Hedera helix)*. This square table arrangement is built on a square board of fresh floral foam. A five-wick black cube candle from Scandinavia has been placed in the centre of the foam.

DETAILS OF DISPLAY
BRIGHT YELLOW
12 Gerbera jamesonii 'Esperanza'
15 Tagetes erecta 'Promise Yellow'
(Afro-French Marigold)
20 Rosa 'Sphinx'
12 Zantedeschia aethiopica
'Florex Gold' (Calla lily)
CHOCOLATE BROWN
30 Rubdbeckia hirta
(Rudbeckia seedheads)
DARK GREEN
12 Hedera helix (Fruiting ivy)

Other flower choices

BRIGHT YELLOW
Achillea 'Moonshine'
Helianthus annus 'Teddy Bear'
(Sunflower)
Rosa 'Taxi'
CHOCOLATE BROWN
Echinacea purpurea
Zea mays (Indian corn)
DARK GREEN
Laurus nobilis
Ruscus hypophyllum

The architectural stature of heliconias and their striking flame red colouring make them popular with party planners and hoteliers as their presence cannot fail to impress.

LOBSTER CLAWS

Native to the American tropics, they inspire towering displays filled with exotic waxy flowers and two-tone reeds.

Heliconias are principally grown in Central Mexico, South America, Hawaii and the Caribbean. They are harvested as cut flowers when mature and are available in either erect or hanging forms. Most heliconias on sale in the UK are imported from Costa Rica and Trinidad but because their long stems are heavy they are expensive to air-freight and this keeps their market price high. But the benefit of buying heliconias is that they make long-lasting and reliable flower displays – the flowerheads do not change form or decompose with age but remain intact until the stems discolour. Heliconias are ideal for locations where the flowers are required to last for up to two weeks. This makes them a favourite for corporate offices, restaurant receptions and hotel entrance displays.

The markings on these 'Lobster Claw' heliconias inspired me to create a strongly coordinated two-tone scheme, using 'Lobster Claw's' distinctive red and lime-green colouring. To create this display, first place the reeds in a tall glass vase and arrange the heliconias in the middle of the reeds. Next add water to the vase, before weaving the shorter-stemmed anthurium flower stems through the heliconias and reeds. Anthurium flowers originate from Columbia. Today they are cultivated in most flower-growing countries and are available in over fifty shades.

DETAILS OF DISPLAY

FLAME RED
5 *Heliconia bihai* 'Lobster Claw'
LIME GREEN
12 *Anthurium* 'Midori'
RUST
30 *Cannomois virgata* (Reeds)

Other flower choices

FLAME RED
Alpinia purpurata (Red ginger)
Gladiolus 'Addi'

LIME GREEN
Anthurium 'Pistache!'
Dendranthema 'Shamrock'
Leucodendron laureolum

RUST
Betula species (Birch stems)
Chamaedorea sefrizii (Reed palm)
Rhodocoma gigantea (Mikado stems)

Thamnochortus insignis (Thatch reed)

BLADE OF GRASS

I am not alone in my fascination for grasses and especially grasses in seed. I like the sense of movement grass meadows bring to the landscape and how, in a similar way, a few strands of grass can lift and lighten a floral display by creating a green halo effect around the feature flowers.

Some of the outdoor pleasures people often describe are the appearance of a wild grass meadow swaying in the breeze or the evocative smell of freshly cut grass. Many of us have a special fondness for grass and I have drawn on this natural pleasure to create this display. When you look carefully at an individual blade of grass, the detail in its structure is astounding. Grasses are very complex plants and the seedhead, for example, is really a flowerhead with a number of distinct parts. Grasses are a diverse group of plants and include both annuals and perennials. They are found in almost every type of natural habitat.

Perhaps the most amazing characteristic of grass is that it grows continuously from the base of the stem so that when it is grazed, harvested, or mowed it quickly produces new plant material. In this delicate hand-tied bouquet, the young green fountain grass (*Panicum virgatum* 'Fountain') sets off the pale pink rose (*Rosa* 'St Celia') and the dusky pink tea rose (*Rosa* 'Julia'). The grass gives the arrangement a light, wispy effect. I have also used snowberries (*Symphoricarpus albus* 'White Pearl'), to help add shape and texture when putting the flowers together in a hand-tied bouquet.

A number of grasses are grown commercially and are available to the florist from early summer to autumn. These include millet grass (*Panicum miliaceum*), which was originally cultivated for bird seed mixtures. Millet grass makes excellent informal foliage for hand-tied bunches and arrangements. I am also very fond of hairy finger grass (*Digitaria sanguinalis*) and the shorter dog's tooth grass (*Dicanthium ischaemum*). Both make precious fillers for flower arrangements.

DETAILS OF THE DISPLAY

PINK
12 *Rosa* 'St Celia'
12 *Rosa* 'Julia'
LIGHT GREEN
20 *Panicum virgatum* 'Fountain' (Fountain grass)
5 *Viburnum opulus* (Guelder rose)
WHITE
10 *Symphoricarpos albus* 'White Pearl'

Other flower choices

PALE PINK
Rosa 'Candy Bianca'
BEIGE
Rosa 'Peppermint'
LIME GREEN
Alchemilla mollis (Lady's mantle)
PALE GREEN
Pennisetum villosum (Wild grass)
Triticum durum (Durum wheat)
WHITE
Ageratum 'Estafette'
Ammi majus (Queen Anne's Lace)
Ascelpias 'Moby Dick'
Lysimachia clethroides

Coordinated arrangements may take a two-tone colour theme from one stunning variegated flower as the starting point. Here, the coloured throats of lime-green cymbidium orchids are speckled with hints of burgundy and pink, and this singing colour mix forms the basis for the display.

ORCHID EXOTICA

This simple Asian style of display, arranged in a glass cube on a flat sushi dish is influenced by the floral work of Thai people that I saw first hand on a trip to Thailand. Here the lime-green cymbidium orchid 'Alice Anderson' – one of my favourites – seemed a good choice. It helps to lift the dark, almost black 'Black Baccarra' roses and bluish-black viburnum berries. The exotic nature of orchids is appropriate to the East-West style and their two-tone colouring suggested a deep red and lime-green theme. To strengthen my East-meets-West design, I decided to use sculptural lotus seedheads (*Nelumbo nucifera*) and spiky coral fern (*Glenchenia polypodiodes*) to add more unusual eastern foliage textures to the display. In true Asian style, I have also woven flax leaves (*Phormium tenax*) to make a decorative basket weave within the glass cube container. The woven flax leaves also hide the floral foam and flower stems from view.

To weave the flax, lay five stems vertically on a flat surface and weave five horizontal stems through the verticals to create a flat woven mat. Flax leaves are flexible but strong and should be fairly easy to weave but to make the task simpler, you can staple the bottom row to hold the verticals in place. When you have completed four mats, trim them to size and place them on each side of the glass cube container. Add soaked floral foam and you are ready for your exotic flower combination.

DETAILS OF THE DISPLAY

DARK RED
9 *Rosa* 'Black Baccara'
9 *Rosa* 'Extase'
LIME GREEN
3 *Anthurium* 'General'
1 *Cymbidium* 'Alice Anderson'
DARK GREEN
10 *Gleichenia polypodiodes* (Coral fern)
5 *Nelumbo nucifera* (Lotus seedheads)
30 *Phormium tenax* (Flax leaves)
BLACK
5 *Viburnum tinus* berries

Other flower choices

DARK RED
Rosa 'Black Magic'
LIME GREEN
Anthurium 'Midori'
Leucadendron platyspermum
DARK GREEN
Asparagus setaceus 'Plumosus'
BLACK
Ligustrum vulgare (Privet berries)

SIMPLE LILIES

*The shape
and subtle colour
of this bloom, with its
simple transition from stem
to flower, makes it a true
muse. It has influenced artists,
architects and designers from Art
Nouveau to the present day.*

The calla lily, originally from Africa, is a true designer's flower in all senses of the word. Floral designers love them because they look as comfortable trailing down in a wedding bouquet as they do upright in a vase arrangement. Their clean lines make them a favourite of architects when displayed in contemporary interiors. This arrangement gives restraint and opulence in the same vase – a winning combination. The strength of colour of the yellow flowerheads is balanced by the mid-green stems and the solid dark green border of reed (*Equisetum giganteum*). Both calla lilies and reeds have an upright growing habit and this straight growth has determined the style of the display. This arrangement is constructed by filling a large glass tank with soaked floral foam and leaving space around the outer edge to create a border of reed stems. Then cut the lilies to one length and fasten a band of florist's tape to the base of each stem to reinforce the ends and prevent the long stems from splitting. Insert the lilies in the floral foam, working from one end of the tank to the other. Move the display into position and top up the tank with water mixed with flower food. The arrangement should last for up to three weeks.

DETAILS OF THE DISPLAY

YELLOW
200 *Zantedeschia aethiopica*
'Florex Gold' (Calla lily)
GREEN
10 *Equisetum giganteum* (Reed)

Other flower choices

YELLOW
Eremurus stenophyllus
(Foxtail lily)
Lilium 'Dreamland'
GREEN
Phyllostachys bambusoides
(Bamboo)

HOT PEPPERS

These red, green and yellow jalapeno chillies were destined for the kitchen when I saw them but I was so taken by their clashing colours that I decided to use them as the focus of a hot table arrangement for a dinner party.

Whenever I am travelling, I always make a point of visiting the local food markets. This fascination for fresh produce extends to my working life in London where fruit and vegetables provide a source of colourful material for my flower displays, particularly over the winter months when the available colour palette of flowers falls off significantly. Fresh and dried chillies have become increasingly popular as a source of colour and shape for the flower arranger in recent years. They are now grown on the stem and sold in the autumn solely for flower decorations. There are dozens of different chillies with different degrees of fieriness and when handled one should avoid contact with the eyes or the skin – they may cause irritation. Here, I have chosen to use fresh jalapeno chillies which start out green and then turn yellow and red as they ripen. This multi-coloured mix of chillies encouraged me to put together a rather unusual combination of flowers. When working with strong colours it is important to balance the colour elements so that one hue does not dominate the rest. In this arrangement, I was able to do this without using any dark green foliage to tone and blend the flower colours because the dark brown of the sunflowers acted as calming influence on the scorchingly loud colours of the bright pink and orange roses and red gloriosa and nerines.

DETAILS OF THE DISPLAY

BRIGHT PINK
3 *Gloriosa rothschildiana*
9 *Rosa* 'Milano'
RED
25 *Capsicum annum* (Peppers)
6 *Celosia argentea* 'Toorts Wijnrood'
3 *Nerine* 'Corusca Major'
YELLOW
25 *Capsicum annum* (Peppers)
5 *Helianthus debilis* subsp. *cucumerifolius*
'Italian White' (Sunflower)
5 *Rosa* 'Ambience'
ORANGE
5 *Rosa* 'Trixx!'
LIME GREEN
7 *Alchemilla mollis* (Lady's mantle)
DARK GREEN
5 *Hedera helix*
BLACK
5 *Rosa* 'Black Baccara'

Other flower choices
BRIGHT PINK
Rosa 'Jacaranda'
RED
Anemone coronaria 'Jerusalem
Red'
YELLOW
Achillea 'Moonshine'
ORANGE
Calendula officinalis (Marigold)
LIME GREEN
Viburnum opulus (Guelder rose)
DARK GREEN
Ruscus hypophyllum
BLACK
Rosa 'Black Beauty'

BLOWSY BLOOMS

The rounded, soft mound of hydrangea flowerheads offers a perfect natural shape for a circular table decoration. On close inspection, each individual floret within the flowerhead displays a mix of pink and lilac tones and makes this blowsy bloom the perfect match for summer pinks and purples.

Until recently, hydrangeas were only available to florists as pot plants. But in the last five years hydrangeas as cut flowers have become available at wholesale flower markets. These new cut flower hybrids last much longer than hydrangeas harvested from the garden and have increased the use of the flower in floral displays. The size of the flowerheads means that hydrangeas will make an impact in large scale arrangements. To prevent the big hydrangea flowerheads dominating, and to create a balanced display, arrange the accompanying smaller flowers in groups so that they occupy the same space as a single hydrangea head. Here, a round, low display of hydrangeas, roses peonies, anemones, celosia and lilac makes an arresting dinner table centrepiece. To create the display, tape a layer of soaked fresh floral foam to the dish to anchor the cut flower stems and keep them well watered. Hydrangeas are thirsty flowers and require plenty of water. Condition all the flowers well before placing them in floral foam. If the hydrangeas start to wilt, try submerging the flowerheads in water to rehydrate the blooms.

DETAILS OF THE DISPLAY

PINK
3 *Celosia argentea* 'Martine Rose'
3 *Paeonia* 'Dr. Alexander Fleming'
6 *Rosa* 'Aqua!'

SKY BLUE
5 *Hydrangea macrophylla* 'Blue Bonnet'

LILAC
5 *Syringa vulgaris* 'Ruhm von
Horstenstein' (Lilac)

ROYAL PURPLE
10 *Anemone coronaria* 'Mona Lisa Blue'

Other flower choices

PINK
Gerbera jamesonii 'Serena'
Rosa 'Purple Cezanne'

SKY BLUE
Echinopsis bannaticus
(Globe thistle)
Hyacinthus orientalis 'Delft Blue'

ROYAL PURPLE
Eustoma russelianum
'Kyoto Purple' (Lisianthus)

When working with seasonal plant material, the first sign of spring – like these old-fashioned tulip varieties sold with their bulbs – is very uplifting. The long, elegant line of the tulip stems with their perfect green leaves, golden brown bulbs and bright-coloured petals are the inspiration for this arrangement.

TULIP BULBS

Bulbs rarely get the chance to star in floral displays but here both roots and bulbs are on show, as interest in how plants grow has increased. Using the growing flower stem with the bulb and roots intact rather than just the cut flower also suggests new ideas for working with old-fashioned favourites, like tulips. The flower display it inspires is naturalistic and informal, presenting the tulips as they are seen growing in nature. Here 'Exotic Bird' tulips, vivid pink 'Anne Marie' gerbera, and japonica foliage (*Chaenomeles japonica*) have been brought together (they are seasonally compatible). To create the display a jumbo block of fresh floral foam – about the size of six standard blocks – has been placed on a shallow dish. Groups of tulips and bulbs have been wired into the base. Then clumps of moss have been pinned onto the foam to hide the base. Gerbera stems are trimmed to different heights for visual interest before branches of japonica are inserted. If the flowers are well-conditioned they will last for up to six days. Mist the bulbs with water to prevent them from drying out.

DETAILS OF
THE DISPLAY

BRIGHT PINK
25 *Chaenomeles japonica*
(Japonica)
25 *Gerbera jamesonni*
'Anne Marie'
150 *Tulipa* 'Exotic Bird'

Other flower choices
BRIGHT PINK
Hyacinthus orientalis
'Jan Bos'
Gerbera jamesonni
'Woy-Woy'
Lilium longiflorum 'Acapulco'
Nerine bowdenii 'Favoriet'
Prunus persica (Cherry
blossom)
Tulipa 'Angelique'

The fiery colour mix and interesting way that oriental bittersweet berries seem to spiral around their stems forms the starting point for this autumnal display, where flowers, leaves and berries are woven together in a rich tapestry of colour.

BRIGHT BERRIES

This still life design uses flowers, branches, leaves and berries to create a rust-coloured landscape of trees, bushes and ground cover. 'Baynard' gerbera flowers have tall stems and create a canopy high above the rest of the display. The arrangement is built on 'designer board' – one side is polystyrene and the other has a layer of floral foam. Cut the board to make a 50cm (20in) square. Soak the foliage in water to condition it before use.

Other flower choices
RUST
Helianthus annus 'Prado Red' (Sunflower)
Gerbera jamesonii 'Lynx'
Pyracantha 'Golden Charmer' (Cotoneaster berries)
Quercus coccinea (Scarlet oak leaves)
PLUM
Berberis thunbergii 'Rose Glow'
GREEN
Papaver orientalis (Poppy seedhead)

Meanwhile, trim the cinnamon sticks to 10cm (4in) long and glue them around the edge of the designer board. Cinnamon sticks add a scented wintry flavour to the arrangement. When the cinnamon sticks are secure, begin covering the whole surface of floral foam with foliage. Use sprigs of beech leaves, fruiting ivy and green dill. Trim the rose stems to about 5cm (2in) and place them among the foliage. Put branches of oriental bittersweet berries among the leaves. Arrange the berried branches so they look natural and appear to be growing wild – twisted through the leaves. Next add the square candles in cinnamon, chocolate and coffee colours. Attach three bamboo prongs around the base of each candle and hold them in place with florist's tape. Insert the prongs into the foam to hold the candles in position. Then add the stems of rust-coloured 'Baynard' gerbera, and finally a twist more of the oriental bittersweet berries to offset the vertical emphasis of the gerbera stems.

DETAILS OF
THE DISPLAY

RUST
10 Celastrus orbiculatus
(Oriental bittersweet)
5 Fagus sylvatica
(Beech leaves)
9 Gerbera jamesonii
'Baynard'
15 Rosa 'Leonardis'
PLUM
10 Cotinus coggygria
f. purpurea
GREEN
Anethum graveolens (Dill)
Hedera helix (Fruiting ivy)

FRESH GREENS

I enjoy the simplicity of mixing fresh green foliage with white flowers. Here, the green-edged white petals of the cabbage rose 'Avalanche' were the starting point for this abundant basket urn brimming with ornamental cabbages, white flowers and other textured material.

Many late summer and autumn flowers and foliages are very textural and invite flower arrangers to put together rich combinations that resemble heavily embroidered tapestries. For this basket, I have chosen lime-green celosia (which has a velvety texture similar to chenille), chunky poppy seedheads, crabapples, millet grass and trailing ivy. Multi-petalled white roses and dahlias lift the surrounding foliage colours and add soft shapes.

The trend in floristry for using long-stemmed fruits and vegetables in displays has encouraged growers to produce decorative fruit and vegetables specifically for sale in the wholesale flower markets. Until quite recently, ornamental cabbages were only available as potted plants. The cabbages were cut off their root system and used in low massed displays or kept in their pots and used in huge pedestal arrangements. The growth in popularity of ornamental cabbages has meant that they are now available as cut flowers from late summer until spring. The rosettes of leaves make a good focal point for arrangements as well as effective fillers. Cabbages are very long lasting and suit a number of different designs from informal rustic baskets to larger and more formal vase and pedestal arrangements. Here, the cut cabbage rosettes have been used in pairs, while elaborate groupings containing a mixture of flowers and foliage help produce a patchwork effect.

DETAILS OF THE DISPLAY

WHITE
10 *Dahlia* 'Karma Serena'
10 *Rosa* 'Avalanche'
CREAM
10 *Brassica oleracea*
(Ornamental cabbage)
GREEN
5 *Celosia argentea*
'Bombay Green'
12 *Hedera helix* species
(Trailing ivy)
10 *Papaver somniferum*
'Hen and Chicken'
(Opium poppy seedhead)
7 *Skimmia confusa*
'Kew Green'
10 *Panicum miliaceum*
(Millet grass)
YELLOW
3 *Malus* 'Butterball'
CHOCOLATE BROWN
7 *Fagus sylvatica* sprigs
(Glycerined beech leaves)

Other flower choices
WHITE
Gerbera jamesonii
'Bianca'
Rosa 'Akito'
CREAM
Achillea 'Big Smile'
Hydrangea paniculata
'Kyushu'

GREEN
Nelumbo nucifera
YELLOW
Craspedia uniflora
PLUM
Berberis thunbergii
'Rose Glow'

Forget-me-nots are very small but when seen in nature in meadows or woodland, their combination of sky blue petals with bright yellow centres makes a memorable colour fusion. This classic mix of blue and yellow is present in many spring flowers and makes a winning combination for any display.

WOODLAND SCENE

The colour union of blue and yellow works particularly well in early spring when iris, tulips and narcissi are in season. All these spring flowers look stunning mixed with early spring-branching foliage. I also turn to this uplifting combination in late summer when yellows and blues are even brighter and deeper and gardens are brimming with sunflowers, delphiniums, globe thistles and eryngium.

In the countryside, early signs that milder spring weather is on the way are the appearance of pale yellow primroses on mossy banks, and the budding branches of birch trees. These indicators of spring are the inspiration for this tablescape. The flowers are arranged in small clusters, as though growing in a woodland setting, with moss and birch twigs forming the foundation of the display. This tablescape is a clever mix of plants and cut flowers arranged on designer board so that the cut flowers are able to drink from the foam, while the plant roots – lifted from their pots – can be kept moist too. Once the designer board has been cut to size, birch twigs are wired together in groups and inserted into the edge of the foam. Carpet moss is then laid over the foam to hide the base. The primrose plants are planted in groups through the display and then the cut flowers including forget-me-nots, grape hyacinths and daffodils are inserted into the foam base in naturalistic groups.

DETAILS OF THE DISPLAY

SKY BLUE
50 *Muscari armeniacum*
'Blue Dream' (Grape hyacinth)
30 *Myosotis sylvatica*
(Forget-me-not)
BRIGHT YELLOW
20 *Narcissus* 'Dick Wilden'
(Double daffodils)
6 *Primula*
'Prominent Series' plants
BROWN
3 branches *Betula pendula*
(Silver birch)
Mnium hornum (Carpet moss)

Other flower choices

SKY BLUE
Hyacinthoides hispanica
'Excelsior'
Triteleia 'Corrina'
BRIGHT YELLOW
Tulipa 'Monte Carlo'
Ranunculus 'Ranobelle Inra
Picotee Geel'
BROWN
Myrica gale

Foliage
Combinations

PRUNUS PERSICA

ALCHEMILLA MOLLIS

PHYTOLACCA AMERICANA

VIBURNUM OPULUS BERRIES

ACACIA RETINODES

ASPARGUS SMILAX

FAGUS SYLVATICA

MNIUM HORNUM

MAGNOLIA SPRENGERI

STACHYS BYZANTINA

CROCOSMIA LEAVES

PSEUDOTSUGA MENZIESII

HAMAMELIS X INTERMEDIA

HOSTA SPECIES

QUERCUS SPECIES

LIGUSTRUM OVALIFOLIUM

CYTISUS MULTIFLORUS

RESEDA LUTEOLA

PHOTINIA X FRASERI 'RED ROBIN'

ILEX SPECIES

In my floral work foliage is an integral part of the design. Like an artist deciding on the background colour of paint on canvas, so the flower arranger must choose the foliage material to form the background from which the arrangement will stand out.

Foliage is important for introducing structure, shape and balance to a display. It can physically 'weave' together flower stems in an arrangement and hold the plant material in position. Even the recent trend for 'all one type' flower arrangements calls for judicious use of foliage. It may be a collar of leaves, a few grasses to lighten the posy or twigs worked through the design to give it height. But foliage is crucial when working with colour because of its ability to help the display work by raising or lowering the temperature. I like to compare the use of foliage in floral displays to turning up or down the colour contrast on a television set. Dark foliage is the safest option and works well with very brightly coloured one-flower arrangements. With mixed flower colours, I prefer to use at least three types of foliage. These may include a fruiting foliage with berries, such as hypericum, sculptural foliage like eucalyptus, and a good edging leaf like aspidistra. I prefer to avoid variegated foliage. It does little to enhance flower colour and seems only to compete for attention with a chosen scheme. I restrict the use of variegated foliage to 'all-foliage' assemblies, such as Christmas wreaths where variegated leaf colour will sit comfortably with other foliage on show. Remember that if you cannot find foliage to complement your choice of flowers, then it is best to use none at all.

Commercially grown foliage

Foliage for use in professional floristry is grown commercially all over the world and much of it is flown in by air-freight, which has a bearing on the cost. Single stems of exotic foliage from South Africa or the tropics can be as expensive as flowers and really beautiful foliage is often a lot more expensive. Much of the more common foliage seen in UK wholesale flower markets, such as bear grass and aspidistra leaves, is grown in Israel and Florida. When choosing a bouquet, it is important not to overlook the costs of foliage in the price. People often expect foliage to be free as they follow the logic that greenery is abundant in nature and therefore available to all. In my own arrangements, foliage is a significant part of the costs, and accounts for at least a quarter of our budget. At least 25 per cent of our hand-tied bouquets are made of foliage, and more for largescale displays.

Seasonal colour choice

Whenever possible, I like to use seasonal native foliage. In spring in the UK, there are a number of wonderful flowering foliages available, including guelder rose (*Viburnum opulus*), spiraea (*Spiraea* x *vanhouttei*) and philadelphus (*Philadelphus* 'Virginal') – a wonderful fragrant but short-lived foliage – and pieris (*Pieris japonica*) with its clusters of drooping jewel-like white flowers. When cut, this spring foliage presents the flower designer with a wonderful fresh new palette of colour to work with. Later in the summer, I turn to grey-blue foliage, such as the herb rue (*Rue graveolens*), ornamental grasses including blue fescue (*Festuca glauca*), or the blue-grey leaves of hosta (*Hosta glauca* 'Elegans'). In summer, several plants with silver foliage including senecio (*Senecio cineraria*), santolina (*Santolina chamaecyparissus*) and verbascum (*Verbascum olympicum*) produce bright yellow flowers and this offers the perfect cue to the florist for a flower colour that works with silver foliage. Yellow strengthens the silver of the foliage.

In autumn, the rich dark foliages of smoke bush (*Cotinus coggygria*), beech leaves (*Fagus sylvatica*) and photina (Photina x *fraseri* 'Red Robin') mix well with a host of bright orange flowers and fruits. Later in the season, the orange and red berries of cotoneaster and chillies add fiery colour to harvest bunches and displays.

In winter, foliage takes centre stage as flowers become more scarce in nature and more expensive to buy. At this time of year, I turn to pure foliage displays which bring together ivy, holly, spruce and mistletoe with other plant material including lichen-covered bare branches, silvery moss and pine cones to add colour and textural interest. Most evergreen foliages are long-lasting when cut and therefore economical to use in displays. They will survive for several weeks if placed in water, which should see you happily through the whole of the festive season and beyond.

Left This spring through to winter selection represents just a few of my favourite foliages. Spring-branching foliage like cherry blossom (*Prunus persica*) looks fabulous massed together in a simple basket, while lime-green summer foliage like lady's mantle (*Alchemilla mollis*), brightens and lifts adjacent flower colours. Trailing autumn foliage, for example, phytolacca (*Phytolacca americana*) adds movement to displays, while autumn berries contribute an opulent effect. In winter, holly (*Ilex* species) become the staple foliage for many festive arrangements.

1

2

3

4

WRAPAROUND FOLIAGE

Wraparound foliage has become a trademark of my flower arranging style. It started when I began to glue or bind small, simple leaves around glass tumblers and jars in a desire to control the entire look of the display – including the container. Having designed arrangements with foliage 'growing' around the outside of the vase in a relaxed, naturalistic way, I moved with the fashion in floristry for more formal designs, using a hot glue gun to attach large sculptural leaves, seedheads and fruit to the outside of vases in regimented patterns. Influenced by the East, I also placed woven mats of flax leaves (*Phormium tenax*) within glass cubes and created rigid square frameworks for flowers using bunches of reed stems tied with raffia (sometimes these plaited reed containers can be bought ready-made). These 'living vases' of wraparound foliage with their skillfully woven leaves can make an excellent starting point for a contemporary display and can be used over again for different flower combinations.

Rose chessboard

The inspiration for this checkerboard design came from a black-and-white themed party for a draughts-playing enthusiast. The design has a masculine restraint and is ideal for a party table as people can talk across it. To create this display, cut a square block of fresh floral foam and place it on a flat Japanese-style dish. Bind four bunches of reed stems (*Equisetum giganteum*) around the base and tie them with raffia. To create a symmetrical display, carefully select roses with the same-sized flowerheads. I used 18 deep red roses (*Rosa* 'Black Magic') and 18 white roses (*Rosa* 'Akito').

| 1 |
Foliage: 6-10 bunches lavender (*Lavandula augustifolia* 'Hidcote'). Flowers: yellow rose (*Rosa* 'Frisco'), bright pink rose (*Rosa* 'Ravel'). Trim down the lavender stems to 5cm (2in) lengths and pin them around a block of fresh floral foam about 4cm (1½in) high. Tie the strands of raffia around the stems to hide the pins. Cut the rose stems to 5cm (2in) and arrange the pink roses in the centre and yellow on the outer edge.

| 2 |
Foliage: 30 stems lamb's ears (*Stachys byzantina*). Using full-length stems, bind the lamb's ears around a glass vase with fine silver wire. This silver-grey wraparound foliage works well when tied around vases of pastel-coloured ranunculus, pale-coloured tulips and garden roses. Globe thistle (*Echinops bannaticus*) and sea holly (*Eryngium alpinum*) also make suitable wraparound plant material.

| 3 |
Foliage: You will need about 30 stems of flax (*Phormium tenax*) for a 16cm (6½in) high square glass container. This leaf-weaving technique is inspired by the Asian tradition. Lay four stems vertically on a flat surface and then weave through the horizontal stems. To secure the stems in place, staple them at the top and bottom. Use this disciplined foliage with extravagant flowers such as orchids, peonies or roses.

| 4 |
Foliage and fruit: 4 long stems old man's beard (*Clematis vitalba*) and 20 limes. Flowers: 15 pale pink peonies (*Paeonia* 'Sarah Bernhardt') 5 deep pink peonies (*Paeonia* 'Pink Panther'), 9 deep pink roses (*Rosa* 'Purple Cezanne'), 9 pale pink roses (*Rosa* 'Anna'). Loosely wrap the trailing foliage around the circular dish, inserting the stem ends in the fresh floral foam to prevent the foliage from wilting.

Living vase display

Using a 25cm (10in) high plastic florist's vase with a stabilizing base, fasten each fruiting ivy leaf to the plastic container with double-sided sticky tape or a specialist flower and foliage glue. Make sure that the leaves overlap and are secure. They will remain fresh for about five days. Then, using about 30 stems of belladonna lilies (*Amaryllis belladonna*), arrange the long flower stems in the hand and trim all the stems to the same length before placing them in the vase. These long-stemmed autumn-flowering bulbs are originally from South Africa and work well as cut flowers in tall displays. For a similar effect, you could use nerines or agapanthus.

1

Scabious seedheads can be gathered from meadows in late summer and are popular for winter dried flower arrangements. They are highly prized for their interesting texture and colour which work well in bouquets. They can also be bought commerically as *Scabiosa stellata* 'Ping Pong'. Here, I have used a hot glue gun to fix a three-deep layer of seedheads to a straight-sided plastic bowl. I have then filled the bowl with fresh floral foam and arranged dried scabious stems in a natural growing style. Lastly, I have sprinkled miniature shells around the base to hide the foam.

2

Remove the individual leaves from the plant stem of each silver tree protea (*Leucodendron argenteum*). You will need about five stems to cover a 25cm (10in) high plastic florist's vase. Fasten the stems in place with florist's glue or double-sided sticky tape. Anemones, hydrangeas, peonies or roses all work well in this display.

3

Sometimes you can purchase ready-made plaited reed containers from Thailand and Singapore to form the base of your arrangement. These containers are usually made from flax (*Phormium tenax*) or other flexible reeds.

4

Here, a simple hand-tied bunch contains lilac-pink roses (*Rosa* 'Blue Curiosa'), gypsophila (*Gypsophila* 'Million Stars') and green trails of ivy stems (*Hedera helix*). The ivy has been grown commercially undercover to keep the stems flexible. The ivy foliage is wrapped in a spiral to give the display movement when viewed from above.

Other ideas for wraparound foliage

☐ Most leaves can be glued to containers but glossy leaves such as laurel, rhododendron and galax will last longer than most. Always use a fabric glue or one made specially for the florist trade. Avoid using a hot glue gun because the heat will scorch the leaves.

☐ For dried flower arrangements, you can buy preserved magnolia leaves which are available in shades of deep burgundy or dark green. Magnolia has a tough, glossy leaf surface while the underside has a texture similar to suede so you can use a hot glue gun to secure the leaves without damaging them.

☐ Seedheads like scabious (shown opposite) can be glued on to plastic pots or any dry, clean surface. Vegetables can also be glued on to containers, including halved turnips or fennel bulbs. Leeks, onions and even large flowerheads, such as sunflowers can also be glued in this way.

☐ The best double-sided sticky tape for the florist is sold in DIY stores as carpet tape. You can find a variety of widths and strengths of tape. If you are attaching bunches of foliage such as box, rosemary or heather, use a strong rubber band to help hold the foliage in place while you are working.

1

2 3

After winter, sprouting branches of spring foliage offer fresh plant material to the flower arranger. The young branches of pussy willow, prunus, japonica and dogwood are soft and pliable and can easily be woven into simple wreaths or twisted attractively around the inside or outside of vases. At this time of year, hazel and birch catkins also make tactile additions to tied bunches and spring displays, and long trails of willow look lovely mixed into early spring wedding bouquets.

Pussy willow (*Salix caprea*) is now available from florists for an extended season from winter to spring. I am particularly enthusiastic about the latest green and silver varieties. For young foliage, I choose whiteleaf (*Sorbus aria* 'Lutescens'). This seems to last longer in the vase than others and has the appearance of shot silk plus an amazing silver-green hue.

SPRING FOLIAGE

1

Foliage: Japonica (*Chaenomeles japonica*). Flowers: Purple snake's head fritillary (*Fritillaria meleagris*) and white snake's head fritillary (*Fritillaria meleagris* f. alba).

2

Foliage: White blossom (*Prunus x cistena*). Flowers: Mixed anemones (*Anemone coronaria*), iris (*Iris atropurpurea*).

3

Foliage: Pussy willow (*Salix caprea* 'Silverglow'). Flowers: Long-stemmed 'French' tulips (*Tulipa* Darwin hybrid). Make sure that the foliage and flowers are well-conditioned before use as there is no water in the three glass bowls. The plant material will last out of water for 48 hours, making this display perfect for a special event.

Amaryllis topiary
Foliage: Red dogwood (*Cornus alba elegantissima*), white blossom (*Prunus glandulosa* 'Alboplena'), band willow (*Salix sachalinensis* 'Sekka'), guzmania (*Guzmania lingulata*). Flowers: Bi-coloured amaryllis (*Hippeastrum* 'Apple Blossom'), red tulips (*Tulipa* 'Prominence') and red cestrum (*Cestrum* 'Red Zohar'). For this display, bind five amaryllis stems together at the base of their flowerheads and place them in a glass vase. Then wrap dogwood stems inside the vase around the flower stems to hide them from view.

1

2

3

4

SUMMER FOLIAGE

1
Foliage: Dill (*Anethum graveolens*). Flowers: These miniature roses are often known as *Rosa* 'Serena'. They are available in mixed colours. Arrange the roses in groups of three and then tie the stems together to form a bunch, before placing them in water.

2
Foliage: Queen Anne's lace (*Ammi majus*), lady's mantle (*Alchemilla mollis*), variegated ivy (*Hedera helix* 'Goldchild'). Flowers: Cream rose (*Rosa* 'Alexis'), cream stock (*Matthiola incana* 'Centum Cream'), white lysimachia (*Lysimachia clethroides* 'Helene').

3
Foliage: Flowering mint (*Mentha x piperita* 'Purple Sensation'), snowberries (*Symphoricarpos albus* 'White Pearl'). Flowers: Pink spray rose (*Rosa* 'Doris Rykers'), hybrid white rose (*Rosa* 'Candy Bianca'), old-fashioned garden roses (*Rosa* 'Julia' and *Rosa* "Margaret Merill').

4
Foliage: Flowering mint (*Mentha x piperita* 'Purple Sensation'). Flowers: Lilac ageratum (*Ageratum houstonianum* 'Blue Horizon'), yellow rose (*Rosa* 'Limonia'), pale pink rose (*Rosa* 'Valerie'), bright pink rose (*Rosa* 'Ballet').

At this time of year, there is an abundance of fresh foliage to choose from both in nature and at the florist. My personal favourites include grasses and seedheads which bring an informality to arrangements. For my own summer country wedding, I used ears of corn throughout all the floral displays. Bells of Ireland (*Molucella laevis*) are also useful for adding a shot of lime green to vases and large pedestal displays, while the more delicate lady's mantle (*Alchemilla mollis*) suits table arrangements and nosegays. For late summer celebrations, I turn to vines and hops which can be woven into stunning garlands and arches. At the end of the summer season, I explore the vegetable patch – a great source of interesting and unusual foliage – and work with herbs such as angelica, dill, mint, and rue which add an aromatic flavour to flower designs.

Bridal bouquet
Foliage: Gardenia leaves (*Gardenia augusta* 'Veitchii'), snowberries (*Symphoricarpos albus* 'White Pearl'). Flowers: Cream roses (*Rosa* 'Hollywood'), white lily (*Lilium* 'Pompeii'). Fragrance and colour play a pivotal role in the choice of flowers. Here, sweet-smelling gardenia flowers have been wired through the design as have star-shaped 'Pompeii' lilies with their soft vanilla colouring and scent. Fragrant ivory 'Hollywood' roses are interspersed with the first of the summer season's snowberries, whose naturally arching stems makes the finished bouquet appear both lively and free-flowing.

1

2

3

4

AUTUMN FOLIAGE

At this time of year, a rich palette of orange, red and brown foliage colours are available to the flower arranger and plant material now includes fruiting branches. Personal leafy favourites include fiery orange oak, deep rust beech, and berried branches of cotoneaster, mountain ash and pyracanthus, which add colour and stature to displays. I also love the purple and plum-coloured berries that appear mid-autumn (such as blackberry), which combine well with seasonal flowers like chrysanthemums, zinnias and dahlias.

1
Flowers: Allium (*Allium sphaerocephalon*), chrysanthemum (*Dendranthema indicum*), cockscomb (*Celosia argentea* 'Bombay Purple' Cristata group), carnation (*Dianthus* 'Bookham Fancy') and rose (*Rosa* 'Femma'). Foliage and fruit: Camellia (*Camellia japonica*), skimmia (*Skimmia japonica* 'Confusa Kew Green'), eucalyptus (*Eucalyptus cineraria*), coleus (*Coleus blumei*) and purple-waxed pears.

2
Flowers: Love-in-a-mist (*Nigella damascena* 'Powder Blue'), scabious (*Scabiosa caucasica* 'Clive Greaves'), delphinium (*Delphinium elatum* 'Harlequin'), rose (*Rosa* 'Mystique'), rudbeckia (*Echinacea purpurea*). Foliage: Camellia (*Camellia japonica*), fruiting ivy (*Hedera helix*), beech (*Fagus sylvatica*), cotoneaster (*Cotoneaster salicifolius*) and apple (*Malus* 'Red Sentinel').

3
This stylized fruit tree is constructed from a globe-shaped metal frame attached to a birch branch which forms the tree trunk. The branch is cemented into a flower pot and then placed inside a red glass vase for decorative effect. Foliage: Panama orange (*x citrofortunella microcarpa*). Fruit: Kumquat (*Fortunella japonica*), lady apple (*Malus* species).

4
Foliage: Spanish moss (*Tillandsia usneoides*), fruiting ivy (*Hedera helix*), snowberry (*Symphoricarpos* 'Pink Pearl'), callicarpia (*Callicarpia bodinieri* 'Profusion'), field mushroom (*Agaricus campestris*), spring onion (*Allium cepa*). Flowers: Dahlia (*Dahlia* 'Night Queen'), rose (*Rosa* 'Blue Curiosa'), hydrangea (*Hydrangea macrophylla* 'Blue Bonnet').

Autumn bowl
To make a striking display of mixed autumnal colour, I have filled a glass vase with dark coffee beans to offset the rich seasonal tones of the flowers and foliage. I have chosen the glossy, deep green leaves and red-flowering panicles of skimmia (*Skimmia japonica* 'Rubella'), ochre-yellow honey berries (*Ilex pyramidalis* 'Fructu Luteo') and American oak leaves (*Quercus palustris*). These are mixed with rich purple and green hydrangea heads (*Hydrangea macrophylla* 'Colour Fantasy'), apricot roses (*Rosa* 'Confetti') and burnt rust calla lilies (*Zantedeschia aethiopica* 'Mango').

1
Foliage: Spanish moss (*Tillandsia usneoides*), lichen-covered twigs of European larch (*Larix decidua*), dried banksia (*Banksia praemorsa*). Flowers: cymbidium orchids (*Cymbidium* 'Pyrate'). In winter, larch trees shed their green leaves and the lovely arch shape of the bare branches looks stunning in winter displays.

2
Foliage: Lichen-covered twigs of European larch (*Larix decidua*), coral fern sprayed silver (*Gleichenia polypodiodes*), blue pine (*Abies pinsape* 'Glauca'). In winter, spraying foliage silver can make green fern-like foliage look more interesting.

3
Foliage: Eucalyptus pods (*Eucalyptus globulus*), mistletoe (*Viscum album*), pussy willow (*Salix caprea*). Flowers: Christmas rose (*Helleborus niger*). This advent wreath is made on a 35cm (14in) fresh floral foam ring. All these flowers and foliage have a limited winter season of about two weeks.

Parallel design
Foliage: Mistletoe (*Viscum album*), umbrella fern (*Stricherus flabiartus*), lucky bamboo (*Dracaena sanderiana*). gourds (*Curcubita pepo*). This parallel design works well as a winter table centrepiece. It creates interest without the need for flowers which are more expensive at this time of the year. The fern and mistletoe can be bought in bunches. The display will last for several weeks.

WINTER FOLIAGE

4
Foliage: Senecio (*Senecio greyii*), viburnum berries (*Viburnum tinus*), brunia (*Brunia laevis*). Flowers: Deep red roses (*Rosa* 'Grand Prix'). With hand-tied bouquets, I like to use a mixture of foliage to add both colour and texture. In winter, silver-grey foliage softens the effect of deep red, and the metallic deep purple berries add a jewel-like quality to the display.

During winter, foliage becomes increasingly important to the florist as flowers become more scarce. Silver-grey foliage (including senecio) mixes well with white winter flowers, such as amaryllis (*Hippeastrum* 'Mont Blanc'). Golden variegated foliage, such as *Euonymous fortunei* 'Emerald Gaiety' – which I avoid at other times of the year because it competes with most flower colours – helps to lift winter displays. Blue pine becomes the centrepiece for Christmas celebrations. In winter, I turn to nature to provide berries and seedheads for colour and textural interest. Even bare branches of trees and vines, and clumps of moss can be used creatively in winter decorations. Dried honeysuckle vine is perfect for weaving into wreaths, while dogwood and birch make good flexible stems to weave into garlands or circular shapes.

Accessory
Colour

The vessel which holds the flowers and foliage is a vital part of any display as it provides the water the plant material needs to survive. But beyond its practical value, the size, style and colour of the container sets the mood for the display and influences the choice of plant material.

When choosing flowers for the home, most people have a limited selection of vases and a favourite location for displaying flowers, and they buy flowers to suit the container. For example, a customer may ask for long-stemmed flowers for a tall glass vase which is to be placed on a hall table. Another may have a single stem vase and is looking for just one exquisite bloom.

Choosing a suitable container

When arranging flowers for an event, I choose the flowers first and then select a container that reflects the party theme. For an 'East-meets-West' party, I favour low, open flower forms (such as cymbidium orchids common to eastern culture), and then select shallow trays or dishes that show off the flower shapes to best advantage. Round party tables suit larger displays but guests need to be able to talk to one another across the table, so again displays in low containers work best. The scale and size of the vessel is important to make a grand statement at an entrance. To achieve this, I use a huge vase at least 1m (3ft) tall, and flowers with long stems, such as lilies. For even larger compositions, I move beyond containers altogether and mount flower and foliage material on a chicken-wire column, or attach the material to a topiary shape.

Natural materials

When we see flowers and foliage against container materials such as glass, wood, basketry or ceramics, it influences how we view the flowers. For example, a metal container will enhance flower colours by reflecting them from its metallic surface. Glass has been immensely popular as a container material and particularly in recent years. Originally, glass became popular because for the first time you could see the flower and foliage stems – being able to see the entire structure of the display somehow enhanced the impact. Glass containers have many qualities that are desirable to the florist. They are tough, available in a variety of shapes, sizes and colours and their transparent surface does not interfere or compete for attention with the plant material. A single glass container can be used to create several different styles of arrangement. For example, the interior of a large glass fishbowl can be lined with fruit and moss, and a cylindrical container can sit in the middle to hold the water and flowers. Alternatively, you can arrange a low posy of flowers in the bowl and fill it with coloured water. Or, simply place the flowers within the interior of the glass bowl – without water – to recreate an old-style terrarium or bottle garden for a special occasion.

Ceramics work well as containers for fresh flowers probably because they are made from earth – the flowers' natural growing medium. Ceramic containers, especially those that have been handmade, often have a solid, rustic appearance that suits larger flowers and foliage, like sunflowers, red hot pokers, grasses and artichokes. The finer ceramics that I do use for floral work look attractive filled with meadow flowers.

Synthetic materials

In my opinion, containers made from synthetic materials such as plastic do not work well with plant material. Plastic is not natural and to my eye looks harsh. I prefer to cover up the surface of plastic containers by gluing leaves onto the plastic – or I wrap up the plastic in a beautiful paper or fabric.

One of my favourite ways to add colour and texture to displays is to fashion containers out of leaves and seedheads – many of these natural-style containers can be seen on pages 44-47. Sometimes, instead of ribbon, raffia or string, I use living strands of foliage or twigs to enhance a display.

In floral competitions, the participants are often given a theme such as a film title or a period in history and then have find or make accessories that fit the brief. Sometimes, a single accessory such as a feather will inspire the flower theme for an event. A bride came to me with the idea of using feathers as confetti and from this we built up a theme for her wedding, whereby we accessorized every display with feathers – from the table centrepieces to the button holes and the wedding cake. But a word of warning, however dominant the accessory theme it should not overpower or outshine the flowers.

Page 56 Bi-coloured *Rosa* 'Oranges and Lemons' are arranged loosely in three coloured glass vases placed side by side.
Page 57 Small white calla lilies (*Zantedeschia aethiopica* 'Crystal') have been arranged in a simple bunch with a collar of ostrich feathers.
Left The chocolate colour of the container is enhanced by three rudbeckia seedheads (*Echinacea purpurea*) in a triangle of pale peach *Rosa* 'Mystique' and an outer edge of pink peach *Rosa* 'Sandy Femma'. Low, angular containers are perfect for dinner party tables.
Right Here, pink phaelinopsis orchids 'Tikal', love-lies-bleeding (*Amaranthus caudatus* 'Albiflora'), deep pink lilies (*Lilium orientale* 'Barbaresco'), black edible grapes and ivy (*Hedera erecta*) are bound around a candlelabra to create this celebration display.

Shape and structure
The gun-metal grey tray displays a formal grid of flowers and fruit. The bold pink gerberas and sunflowers rest on top of spiky West Indian gherkins (*Cucumis anguria*), green and yellow jalapeno chillies and blocks of bright pink and acid yellow carnations. The neutral-coloured container combines well with vivid flower colours.

Striped ribbon drum
Taking the colours in the ribbons as my cue, I have created a bright posy of astrantia (*Astrantia major* 'Rosita'), love-in-a-mist (*Nigella damascena* 'Power Blue'), lilac sweet peas (*Lathyrus odoratus*), bright pink dahlias (*Dahlia* 'Karma Fuchsiana'), pink *Amaryllis belladonna*, yellow roses (*Rosa* 'Papillon') and allium (*Allium sphaerocephalon*).

Multiple vases
Rather than just considering one vessel, think about how several containers work as a group. These handmade coloured glass vases were designed to interlock with one another and the flowers have been chosen to match the vase colours. Here, I have selected bold flowers such as hydrangea, dahlia, globe thistle and chrysanthemum.

Natural order
A shallow Japanese lacquered tray is ideal for displaying fruit or individual flowerheads. To reinforce the symmetry, I have chosen similar-sized waxed pears, lined them up in rows and isolated the colours. This controlled way of displaying natural forms is becoming increasingly popular and you can buy containers with compartments to keep elements in perfect lines.

CONTAINER COLOUR

The colour as much as the style of the container can set the tone of the display. Greens and neutral colours from beige to brown, make versatile containers and work well with a whole spectrum of flower and foliage colour. Black, white and grey vessels suit stark and simple interiors and enhance bold primary flower colours and pure whites. I find that blue is a particularly useful container colour and that azure blue vases look stunning filled with tall stems of purple alliums, lilac-coloured hydrangeas and sky blue delphiniums. Blue also works well in more conventional interiors. I like to fill traditional ceramic containers, such as blue-patterned Spode with spring flowers or arrange Wedgewood Jasperware with white garden roses. More difficult to work with are containers in colours which are not commonly found in the plant world, such as turquoise. A solution to difficult colours is to follow a simple white flower theme. As well as plain coloured vases, I'm also drawn to striped and spotted vases which coordinate well with a mix of colourful flowers. I try to avoid busy container patterns which overpower the flowers.

Frosted glass containers
This lime green frosted glass vessel is the perfect counterpoint for fresh flowers. The container colour picks up the green of the dahlia flower buds and creates a harmony with the mixed dahlias in the arrangement. Frosted white and green glass vases are much more versatile than those with vivid colours and patterns.

Painted bucket

Small metal buckets can be transformed to match your choice of flowers with a coat of oil-based paint. To create a packed display of roses and French marigolds, first arrange the flowers in a hand-tied bunch. The current trend is for colourful massed displays where the flowerheads sit just above the edge of the container.

Galvanized metal arrangement

This contemporary low table centrepiece contains a compact display of lime-green tinged 'Avalanche' roses surrounded by a loose collar of kangaroo paw (*Anigozanthus flavidus*). The rose stems are trimmed down to 2.5cm (1in) and packed in rows into a thin layer of fresh floral foam. The subtle colour palette creates a sophisticated flavour.

Soapstone vase

The subtle variations in hue of natural stone surfaces work well with delicate shades of rose petals. First arrange the cluster of roses in the hand to produce a dome shape and then tie the stems together with string just below the flowerheads. Cut the stems so that the roses sit just above the edge of the vase.

Sand-filled cube

Layers of coloured sand can transform the interior of a plain glass cube and present a classic posy of cream roses in a new light. Place a smaller vase inside the cube to hold the flowers and then fill up the cube around the inner vase with waves of sand. Arrange the roses with a collar of glossy green galax leaves. Trim the stems to fit the inner vessel.

Choosing containers

☐ When choosing a container, consider the size of the neck or opening and make sure it is sufficiently large or small for your purposes. The weight of the vessel is also key – too light and it may topple over, too heavy and it may be awkward to place in location.

☐ Clear glass is always popular with the flower arranger because it is unobtrusive and shows off every part of the flower including the stem. A simple tied bunch in a glass vase reveals the structure in all its glory.

☐ Vases that have been designed to work as a group are useful for creating still life displays. In contemporary interiors, I like to use three identical vases and only fill one with flowers or line up a row of vases with only one or two flowers in each vase for minimal style. Colour blocking also produces dramatic results in plain interiors. I like to use groups of vases in distinct colours with bold-coloured flowers to match.

☐ Ceramics containers add interest to floral displays. It can be fun to use modern, angular ceramic plates and low dishes as flower containers to provide new colour and shape for table decorations.

☐ Metal florists' buckets have become popular for display purposes. Shiny metals help to reflect the colour of the flowers. Zinc and galvanized metal are heavy and so make solid containers for large displays. Iron vessels with a surface patina or rust look fabulous with flowers and iron garden urns are great for largescale flower arrangements for celebrations and functions.

☐ Natural or painted wood containers are also an interesting choice. Their grain makes them sympathetic to the flowers but because the wood is not watertight they should be lined with plastic before use. My favourites are flat platters which have a Japanese flavour.

Handblown striped glass vase
A two-tiered arrangement of dahlia (*Dahlia* 'Chinese Lantern') with deep burgundy angelica (*Angelica gigas*) perfectly match the orange and brown tones of the simple vessel.

Cardboard and paper boxes
A simple cardboard box can be used to create a fun carrier-bag style container for a vase of fresh flowers. For a children's party table centrepiece, I glued on a collage of overlapping colour pages from a favourite comic. I chose burgundy and orange ranunculus with pink and purple anemones to create a lively colour display.

FABRICS AND ALTERNATIVES

Fabrics can be used in imaginative ways to make ordinary plant pots and flower vases look more interesting. For example, when I came across some wonderful lampshades made from strips of coloured ribbon at a gift fair, I commissioned the designer to produce some drum-shaped flower vases decorated with ribbon (*see page 60*). Brightly coloured stripes of ribbon are great fun to coordinate with flowers as are Indian sari fabrics which you can find at markets. As well as exploiting vibrant fabric colours, I am also drawn to texture, particularly the rough quality of hessian and other natural woven fabrics, which I wrap around plant pots to bring an informal look to an outdoor party. When a large room needs decorating for a formal celebration, generous swags of fabric interwoven with flowers and foliage make the fresh plant material go further and keep costs down. When commissioned to decorate huge exhibition halls, I often resort to this money-saving technique. Fabric is also useful during the winter months, when flowers are more expensive. However, Christmas brings a wealth of other seasonal decorative accessories. Tall glass vases look wonderful filled with glass balls, and once again ribbon woven into bows or threaded through wreaths and garlands adds interest to plant material.

Sequined flower bag
Fashion handbags make eyecatching fresh flower holders for teenage bridesmaids. The flowers are conditioned in water overnight and then the stems are wrapped in plastic with a small amount of water to keep the bouquet light. Here, deep purple anemones, lilac, guelder rose, and 'Negrita' tulips are arranged with fruiting ivy berries.

Wraparound fabric
Fabrics provide an inexpensive way to transform a container. Luxurious fabrics like velvet and silk add drama to bold flowers while lightweight fabrics suit more delicate flowers. Here a square of purple silk is tied around a glass bowl and pinched into soft folds. Pink peonies, red 'Milano' and dark 'Black Baccara' roses are mixed with calla lilies and lilac.

Bridal posy

This traditional bouquet may look simple but in fact every flower and leaf has been individually wired by an experienced florist. Only top quality calla lilies (*Zantedeschia aethiopica* 'Crystal') have been selected for the bride's posy – without a mark on the petals – and each flower is well conditioned in water before wiring to prevent it from drooping. Once the flowers are in place, the posy is edged with galax leaves and then the wires are cut to a length of about 7.5cm (3in). The wires are then bound with florist's tape. Next, satin ribbon is wound around the tape from the base of the leaf collar to the bottom of the stems to provide a 'handle' for the bride. A simple white satin bow is the only accessory.

Violet nosegay

Violets – as their appearance suggests – are closely related to pansies and have been cultivated for centuries in the South of France and the Italian Riveria for the perfume industry. *Viola odorata* is commonly known as sweet violet and the oil is used for flavouring as well as for scent. Although violets only last a few days as cut flowers, their sweet fragrance makes them very popular. They are unlike many flowers in that they are able to drink through their flowerheads as well as their stems and so benefit from complete submersion in water before they are arranged. Once soaked in water, the flowers will be brighter and fresher and can be tied into a dainty posy. In this simple display, they are secured with an elastic napkin ring decorated with two purple baubles which match the flowerheads.

Zinc cube of carnations

Throughout Europe, carnations are currently undergoing a revival in popularity with flower arrangers. Once considered ordinary, these inexpensive, multi-petalled blooms are ideal for displays that use a mass of one type of flowerhead to create a solid block of colour. Here, a straight-sided metal container is filled with fresh floral foam, and the carnations are added in uniform rows. To hide the gap between the flowers and the top of the container, loose strands of waxed paper ribbon are wound around the neck of the container. If topped up with water this contemporary display should last for up to three weeks.

Fashion accessories

☐ Having been brought up on a poultry farm, I have never been a huge fan of feathers, but they can add fabulous shape, texture and colour to fashion-conscious floral displays. My favourites are dyed marabou feathers which are soft and easy to wire into arrangements and bouquets. White feather boas and strings of feathers also look attractive wound around stems of simple flowers to form a fluffy collar. Natural-coloured feathers in deep browns, chestnuts and black work best with autumn tones and harvest themes. Ribbon and trimming shops often sell feathers so look out for useful examples.

☐ Beads, costume jewellery and cut glass can also be used. Simply thread them onto strands of grass and then wind the grass around the posy, or weave them through the arrangement. Personally, I feel that using jewels with fresh flowers is 'gilding the lily' but there are florists who use them tastefully and successfully in displays.

Feathers and rope
This simple living topiary tree of chocolate cosmos (*Cosmos astrosanguineus*) has been placed into soaked fresh floral foam in a plain ceramic vase. The bases of the flowerheads have been bound together with a length of coir rope, while natural brown feathers hide the foam in the container and make an attractive accessory detail.

FOOD AND FLOWERS

The use of fruit and vegetables with flowers for decoration has many historical precedents. In the UK, the garden flower-arranging tradition encouraged the use of all materials from the garden, including fresh produce from the vegetable plot and orchard. This decorative use of fruit and vegetables influenced garden clubs across the world. In my opinion, fruit and vegetables work well with flowers because they complement natural flower shapes, textures and colours. I find the wealth of home-grown and imported fruit and vegetable material on offer particularly inspiring. In recent years, more plentiful

Assymetrical pumpkin group
Pumpkins make attractive containers for autumn displays. Here, green pumpkins are mixed with berries on branching stems (*Senecio rowleyanus*) and seedheads (*Sparganium erectum*) and four stems of white calla lilies (*Zantedeschia aethiopica* 'White Dream'). To make a pumpkin container, cut out the flesh with a knife and then line the interior with plastic before filling it with water.

supplies of exotic fruits and vegetables have become available which has strengthened the appeal of fresh produce. Fruit and vegetables are particularly useful for florists planning large decorative schemes. Their addition to huge topiary displays, swags or garlands makes flowers and foliage go much further and keeps flower costs down. Fruit and vegetables also come into their own in autumn and winter when there is less flower material available and market prices rise. But, they should really be limited to celebration displays because as the fruit and vegetables start to decay they release ethylene gas which shortens the life of flowers.

Bright blueberry mix

Small berries and soft fruits like redcurrants and blueberries do not deteriorate when submerged in water. Here, a hand-tied bunch of brightly coloured flowers and inedible blue-black *Viburnum tinus* berries are teamed up with fresh blueberries in a glass cube. Both types of berries have a metallic-blue blush which complements the rich flower colours. The flowers used include guelder rose, 'Grand Prix' and 'Deep Secret' roses and orange-pink gloriosa (*Gloriosa rothschildiana*).

Liquorice Allsorts ring

To create a frivolous party theme for the young at heart, I like to pair sweets with flowers. Liquorice Allsorts – a peculiarly English sweet – are some of my favourites, and I once arranged a whole party around these bright pink, blue, yellow and orange sweets. In this display, groups of bold 'sweet-coloured' flowers have been arranged on a floral foam ring around three glass cylinders filled with floating pink candles. Liquorice Allsorts are glued in clusters between the flowerheads. This table centrepiece was originally conceived for a children's birthday party but is also popular with adults. The flowers featured include salmon-pink ranunculus, bright yellow carnations, pink 'Ballet' roses, blue hydrangea heads, spiky red leucospermums, grape hyacinths and the cheerful gerbera 'Elmira' with its pink petals and egg-yolk yellow centre.

Primary colour cube

Flowers dyed in artificial colours are a controversial issue in the flower world but they can be fun. Here, each bright candy-coated chocolate has a rose to match. The natural rose colours include the orange rose 'Naranga', the yellow 'Yellow Island' rose and the red 'Grand Prix' rose. Only the bright green and deep blue roses have been dyed. To create this display, place a glass vase inside the larger cube and fill it with water. Use about 1lb (500g) of miniature chocolates to fill up the cube. The display will last for one week.

Using food in displays

☐ Some larger vegetables and fruits make good natural containers for summer and autumn parties. Watermelons with their pink flesh and dark green skin add colour interest as do pumpkins with their ochre yellow skin. My favourite vegetable as a container is the Savoy cabbage. I love the fresh green leaves at the heart and its suede-like texture especially when paired with white or deep red flowers. It also looks wonderful when the cabbage leaves are spray-painted gold and filled with deep burgundy roses.

☐ Tall, slender vegetables such as leeks and spring onions work well wrapped around tall vases or pots. Simply tie the vegetables in place with string, or glue them in position with a hot glue gun.

☐ For regional celebrations, I like to use native vegetables and flowers. For example, for Scottish events, I use turnips and heather and glue them around plastic pots before filling them with autumnal flowers, such as dahlias and asters.

☐ Fennel and pak choi both have lovely fresh green and white leaves which can add texture to summer basket displays.

☐ Globe artichokes have a fantastic uniformity of design which works well in structured displays. They also make suitable containers for candles and nightlights.

☐ Smaller fruits such as crabapples, cranberries and cherries look good packed into glass vases and, like blueberries, survive well in water. Cranberries in displays are a favourite of mine for Thanksgiving or Christmas.

☐ Small, ornamental vegetables such as chillies, pattypan and miniature aubergines also look good arranged in glass vases.

☐ Fruit and vegetables can help to theme a party. Spring onions and asparagus give a country garden feel. Chillies and peppers add Mexican flavour.

Fresh limes with calla lilies

Lily vases – originally intended for floor-standing displays – are currently popular on buffet or bar tables because they create impact in a large function room or marquee. When making a tall arrangement above head height, try to balance the vertical plant material with horizontals. Here, Bells of Ireland (*Molucella laevis*), red hot pokers (*Kniphofia* 'Alcazar') and trailing green amaranthus (*Amaranthus caudatus* 'Viridis) create the verticals. Lime green anthurium (*Anthurium* 'Midori') and chrysanthemums (*Dendranthema* 'Shamrock'), rust calla lilies (*Zantedeschia aethiopica* 'Mango'), lily grass (*Liriope muscari*) and palm leaves (*Rhapis excelsior*) provide the horizontal balance. The slender vase is filled with at least 30 miniature limes for decoration. These small fruit can be difficult to find so as an alternative use supermarket limes, sliced in half or quartered.

Crabapple tower

Yellow crabapples (*Malus* 'Butterball'), available on the stem or as decorative fruit in punnets from the flower market, have been used to fill this tall cylindrical glass vase and to hide the stems of the flowers and foliage. To create this tiered display, I have used golden yellow roses (*Rosa* 'Tresor 2000'), magnolia leaves (*Magnolia macrophylla*), chocolate cosmos (*Cosmos astrosanguineus*), bulrushes (*Typha latifolia*) and contorted pieces of bamboo. The flowers have been arranged in layers of colour and then edged with a collar of leaves.

Wraparound leeks with amaryllis

Leeks have a beautiful graduation of colour from white roots and stems to green tops, and look wonderful wrapped around this straight-sided vase. To arrange the leeks, place a strong rubber band around the vase and insert the vegetables underneath the band. Once in place, tie the leeks with a heavy rope to prevent them from slipping out. Inside the vase, arrange the bi-coloured amaryllis flowers (*Hippeastrum* 'Minerva') and hairy lime green Ascelpia (*Ascelpia physocarpa* 'Moby Dick').

Gooseberry fruit pot

Tall, straight-stemmed flowers are a good shape for making topiary tree displays. Here, pink nerines have been tied together so that their heads create a ball of flowers and then placed in a pale pink ceramic pot. The flowers have been tied together both under their heads and also at the base of the stems. This makes it easier to place the tree into soaked floral foam without the stems breaking. The gooseberry lookalikes decorating the edge of the pot are, in fact, ornamental gherkins from the West Indies (*Cucumis anguria*) and they hide the foam. If they are not available, use lychees or gooseberries instead.

Seasonal
Colour
Palettes

Despite the huge palette of colours available to the flower arranger through the year, we are led by seasonal colour. In the same way that fruit and vegetables taste better in season, so using the flowers and foliage of the moment has greater visual appeal.

Even with the increasing availability of many flowers all year round, there is no doubt that there is still a strong emphasis on seasonal colour in the flower arranger's calendar. Some flower colours have strong associations with specific seasonal events but often this is due to clever marketing rather than the actual availability of the flowers as today many flowers are grown across the world and, like fruit and vegetables, are available for much of the year.

The intensity of the natural light which changes with the seasons and from one country to the next also influences our choice of flower colour. In Northern Europe, where light levels are low, pale flowers which reflect light are popular. While in the Southern Hemisphere where the light is very intense, hotter colours are preferred.

We tend to associate flower colours with nature and the dominant colour in the landscape at a particular time of year. Pure white is the first colour of the seasonal palette as snowdrops are the earliest plants to flower. Soon after, white crocus, narcissi and tulips come into their own as do flowering branches of white magnolia, dogwood and species of prunus.

Seasonal colour shift

Following early white flowers, shades of yellow are the next most prevalent hue in the floral palette. In early spring, pale yellow primroses and dainty aconites are followed by the more saturated yellows of daffodils and forsythia. The deepest yellow can be seen in the wild blossoms of *Forsythia* 'Beatrix Farrand' or *Narcissus* 'Rembrandt', and spring tulips, like 'Monte Carlo' or 'Yokohama'.

Pale spring yellows mix well with the pale pinks and light blues of the season, while stronger yellows suit other primary-coloured flowers. Many of the yellow spring flowers are bulb flowers and grow to a similar size so they look good displayed together as cut flowers.

As the days become warmer and the number of daylight hours increase, yellow flowers are joined by soft purple and blue flowers in the landscape. Bluebells and wild foxgloves appear in woods and fragant lilacs, grape hyacinths and iris come into bloom in the garden. In the height of summer, there is an explosion of colour. But it is the deep pinks and azure blues which dominate and have become seasonal favourites for summer parties and weddings. Blues and hot pinks are the quintessential mid-summer flower colours. The vibrant summer blues include delphiniums, gentians, cornflowers, agapanthus and veronica, while garden roses and peonies offer a stunningly rich palette of pink shades.

Deep yellow, orange, rust and brown belong to the late summer and autumn. Orange is a late summer colour and comes into its own during the autumn months. It is the colour of Halloween, Harvest Festival and Thanksgiving. Chocolate brown is also autumnal but, like black, it has a fashion cachet and can be used with style through the year.

Purple is an aloof colour with no particular seasonal timing, making an appearance in spring with violets, in the mid-summer garden border with hybrid delphiniums, gladioli, and larkspur and late summer in thistles and ornamental cabbages. Green and silver foliages are also seasonal all-rounders, playing supporting roles to the seasonally inspired flower colour palette.

Other sources of seasonal colour

Fruits and seedheads should not be forgotten for they play a pivotal role in the floral colour palette at the end of the year. In late autumn and winter when there is less plant material available, yellow fruits, such as crabapples and pyracanthus berries help bolster displays. Deep black privet berries and blue-tinged viburnum berries add depth to arrangements and lift reds, oranges as well as purples. Red berries have a strong association with Christmas and rosehips are among my favourites. White fruits are rarer but the one I frequently use is the *Symphoricarpos* 'White Hedge'. As the year unfolds, month-by-month, the flower arranger can select from a huge palette of colours and textures and create harmonious arrangements that reflect the seasons and nature's circle of renewal.

Page 72 Florist's roses, including pale pink *Rosa* 2000, sandy peach *Rosa* 'Sandy Femma', rosy peach *Rosa* 'Femma' and the marmalade-orange *Rosa* 'Trixx!' are mixed with fresh lime fruits and glossy green camellia leaves to produce this summery pastel palette.
Left An autumnal tower of red and yellow crabapples (*Malus* 'Cowichan' and *M.* 'Butterball') are pinned into a dried floral foam cone, using long haberdashery pins. This attractive display of ornamental fruits will last up to three weeks. For Thanksgiving celebrations, I like to make cone-shaped towers with fresh cranberry fruit. Although time-consuming to make, they never fail to impress. *Right* In this display, 'Black Magic' roses have been divided into four groups of three and placed throughout the bouquet. A cluster of bobbly lime-green brunia foliage *(Brunia alopecuroides)* and lime-green celosia (*Celosia argentea* 'Bombay Green') adds texture and contrasts beautifully with the purple leaves of cotinus (*Cotinus coggyria* 'Royal Purple') and the opaque viburnum berries.

SOFT SPRING YELLOWS

Pale creamy yellows combined with fresh leaf greens are the key colours in the early spring palette. Flower petals are fragrant and branching foliage bursts with new life.

HYACINTH WHITE

NARCISSUS CREAM

PRIMROSE YELLOW

DAFFODIL YELLOW

HELLEBORUS GREEN

WEEEPING WILLOW GREEN

CATKIN GREEN

Pale creamy yellows are the essence of early spring. Nature is a great designer – you only have to look at the wild yellow daffodils and soft yellow primroses growing in woodland and on roadside verges for colour inspiration. Early flowering bulbs such as narcissi and hyacinths are also highly fragrant and this is one of the added pleasures of the season. *Narcissus* 'Early Cheer' – featured in this display – is perhaps my favourite. Spring yellows from cream to bright yellow offer an easy palette for the flower arranger as they mix happily with fresh lime-green foliage which is in plentiful supply at this time of year. Here, the delicate frothy globes of guelder rose (*Viburnum opulus*) and the erect stems of pale green hellebores have a sharpness and vibrancy of hue when juxtaposed with the pale yellows of early spring. Black viburnum berries (*Viburnum tinus*) – left over from winter – are also placed in this floral bouquet to add depth and to make the paler plant material appear even lighter and fresher. Create a hand-tied bunch out of these early spring flowers and foliage and place them in a frosted glass vase for maximum appeal.

DETAILS OF THE DISPLAY

3 *Helleborus argutifolius*
20 *Narcissus* 'Early Cheer'
20 *Rosa* 'Evita'
10 *Rosa* 'Jade'
30 *Tulipa* 'Royal Sphinx'
5 *Viburnum opulus* (Guelder rose)
5 *Viburnum tinus* (Berries)

Other flower choices

WHITE
Anemone coronaria 'Mona Lisa White'
Narcissus 'Ziva'

CREAM
Matthiola incana 'Carmen' (Stock)
Rosa 'Hollywood'

PALE YELLOW
Freesia 'Dukaat'
Narcissus 'Fortune'

BRIGHT YELLOW
Rosa 'Aalsmer Gold'
Tulipa 'Monte Carlo'

LIME GREEN
Alchemilla mollis (Lady's mantle)
Euphorbia myrsinites

EARLY SUMMER PASTELS

The pastel shades of pale pinks and blues that dominate flower colour in early summer offer up some of my favourite flower combinations. This classic colour mix has timeless appeal and forms the heart of many summer wedding celebrations and parties.

THISTLE BLUE

DELPHINIUM BLUE

MARSHMALLOW PINK

ROSE PINK

DEEP PEONY PINK

Although a host of pink flowers can be found in the garden and at wholesale flower markets throughout the year, early summer is the moment when the palette of pinks available to the florist and the gardener is at its best. The choice of pink flowers is then truly magnificent and includes phlox, carnations, stocks, foxgloves, sweet peas, campanula, lupins, garden roses and cooler pinks, such as peonies. Cool pink derives from crimson and has a touch of blue in its chromatic make-up which makes it a perfect partner for sky blue flowers, such as delphinium (*Delphinium elata* 'Sky-Liner') as featured in this arrangement. Cool pinks also mix well with other summer blues including cornflowers, love-in-a-mist, agapanthus, meconopsis and scabious. In combination, soft blues and pinks always present a calming, agreeable scheme which is perhaps one reason why this colour union is a key feature of the herbaceous border in a traditional English garden. This two-tiered arrangement tries to recreate the compostion of an herbaceous border in flower. The plant material has been arranged naturalistically as though growing out of the tall vase. A fresh floral foam ring forms the base to anchor the arrangement.

DETAILS OF THE DISPLAY

10 *Ammi majus* (Queen Anne's Lace)
35 *Delphinium elatum* 'Sky-Liner'
5 *Eryngium* 'Orion'
12 *Hedera helix*
10 *Hydrangea macrophylla* 'Blue Tit'
7 *Matricaria capensis* (Feverfew)
20 *Paeonia* 'Dr. Alexander Fleming'
20 *Paeonia* 'Sarah Bernhardt'

Other flower choices

SKY BLUE
Agapanthus 'Donau'
Delphinium belladonna 'Sky Blue'

AZURE BLUE
Delphinium belladonna
'Volkerfrieden'
Gentiana 'Sky'

PASTEL PINK
Eustoma russellianum 'Kyoto Rose
Pink' (Lisianthus)
Rosa 'Candy Bianca'

BRIGHT PINK
Paeonia 'Karl Rosenfield'
Lilium orientale 'Acapulco'

DEEP PINK
Celosia argentea 'Bombay Purple'
Gerbera jamesonii 'Dark Serena'

SUMMER MEADOW

This typical mid-summer palette presents a gentle harnony of cool blue and white with a hint of lilac, while the yellow centres of marguerite daises and asters add a bright accent of colour.

ARTEMISIA GREY

NIGELLA BLUE

SCABIOUS BLUE

BUTTERCUP YELLOW

SWEET PEA PINK

PHLOX PINK

ROSEMARY GREEN

Chrysanthemum daisies (*Chrysanthemum frutescens* 'Comtesse de Chambord') combined with country flowers like love-in-a-mist and scabious, capture the essence of a summer meadow. To reinforce the cool colour harmony of this display, I have used sprigs of grey-green rosemary around the base. In midsummer, there are plenty of silver-grey foliages available to choose from, including artemisia, convolvulus, ornamental artichoke (*Cynara* species) and lamb's ears (*Stachys byzantina*). Silver-grey foliage complements pastel colours – the silver tones amplify and reflect the colours in sunlight. To create this celebration cake display, attach rosemary sprigs to the edge of a straight-sided bowl with double-sided sticky tape. Fill the container with fresh floral foam and then add the flower mix to create a low dome-shaped arrangement. Finish off with a decorative ribbon and candles to match.

DETAILS OF THE DISPLAY

5 *Aster novi-belgii*
'Painted Lady'
(September daisy)
20 *Chrysanthemum frutescens*
'Comtesse de Chambord'
(Marguerite daisy)
10 *Nigella damascena*
'Miss Jekyll' (Love-in-a-mist)
10 *Nigella damascena*
'Power White' (Love-in-a-mist)
10 *Rosmarinus officinalis*
branches *(*Rosemary)
15 *Scabiosa caucasica*
'Clive Greaves' (Scabious)

Other flower choices

SKY BLUE
Hyacinthoides hispanica
'Excelsior' (Bluebell)
Muscari armeniacum 'Bl
Dream' (Grape hyacinth)

LILAC
Freesia 'Castor'
Scabiosa stellata (Scabious)

PASTEL PINK
Chelone obliqua (Turtlehead)
Cirsiun japonicum 'Pink Beauty'
(Plumed thistle)

WHITE
Aster universum 'Monte Casino'
(September daisy)
Matricaria capensis (Feverfew)

As summer ends, I find myself drawn to autumn's golden yellow palette. I enjoy these warm, healing colours before the days shorten and winter sets in.

LATE YELLOWS

In late summer and early autumn, the rich and deep tones of yellow flowers come into their own. In the garden, ochre-yellow flowers like sunflowers, calendulas, chrysanthemums, dahlias and achilleas are evident. Yellow has an uplifting effect on our senses but it can overpower other colours so I like to use it on its own to create arresting and bold monochromatic schemes. If you choose to arrange flowers of one colour, you need to select them for shape and height (contrast round flower shapes with tall) and textural interest. Also, try to use some deep yellow flowers that have a hint of green to exaggerate the pure yellow of others. Here, I have chosen to contrast one tall and one textured yellow flower in each vase. Towering stems of dill *(Anethum graveolens),* foxtail lilies *(Eremurus stenophyllus)* and red hot pokers *(Knipholia* 'Wrexham Buttercup') are set off by collars of sunflowers, roses and celosia to create two-tiered displays. Place the three vases together as a group for an informal summer lunch party.

ACHILLEA YELLOW

WHEAT YELLOW

SUNFLOWER YELLOW

OLD-FASHIONED ROSE YELLOW

CELOSIA YELLOW

GREEN DILL YELLOW

FOXTAIL LILY YELLOW

KANGAROO PAW BROWN

BULRUSH BROWN

DETAILS OF THE DISPLAY

2 *Anethum graveolens* (Dill)
5 *Cannomois virgata* (Lipstick reed)
5 *Helianthus annus* 'Teddy Bear'
(Sunflower)

DETAILS OF THE DISPLAY

10 *Eremurus stenophyllus*
(Foxtail lily)
15 *Rosa* 'Graham Thomas'

DETAILS OF THE DISPLAY

1 *Celosia cristata* 'Bombay Green'
30 *Knipholia* 'Wrexham Buttercup'
(Red hot poker)

RICH HARVEST

Rich, deep colours set the tone for autumnal displays. Here, the colour theme is inspired by the harvested millet and red dogwood stems of the season rather than flower colour.

DAHLIA PLUM

AMARANTHUS GREEN

BLACKBERRY BLACK

BEECH LEAF BROWN

HYPERICUM BERRY RED

DOGWOOD RED

As autumn takes hold, a diversity of sculptural plant material including branches, twigs and leaves becomes available to the flower arranger. The colour palette shifts to dark red and burgundy, adding warmth and depth of colour to end of year displays, particularly when contrasted with brighter flower colours. In addition to strong earthy tones, twigs and branches provide the florist with pliable material to fashion into baskets, containers and wreaths. The autumn flowers I enjoy working with include dahlias, sedums, amaranthus and gladioli. I mix these flowers with berries sold on the stem, including blackberries, spindle berries and callicarpa, or clusters of individual autumn fruits, such as damsons and grapes. Foliage like cotinus and red euphorbia (*Euphorbia griffithii* 'Dixter') work well in combination with dark red gladioli, heliconia (*Helenium* 'Moerheim Beauty') and burgundy dahlias. To create this display, tall stems of red dogwood are tied around a 75cm (30in) glass cylinder and fastened with rope. A hand-tied bunch of dyed black roses are placed in the vase without cutting the stems and a collar of green millet grass is placed loosely around the edge of the roses. Selecting black-coloured roses has the visual effect of making the green grass and red stems appear more vibrant.

Other flower choices

RED
Cornus alba 'Aurea' (Dogwood stems)
Rosa 'Passion'

GREEN
Amaranthus caudatus 'Viridis' (Loves-lies-bleeding)
Panicum virgatum 'Fountain' (Fountain grass)

BLACK
Cornus alba 'Kesselringii' (Dogwood stems)
Tulipa 'Queen of Night'

DETAILS OF THE DISPLAY

40 Cornus alba 'Sibirica' (Dogwood stems)
30 Panicum miliaceum (Millet grass)
40 Rosa 'Black Grand Prix' (Dyed black roses)

AUTUMN BERRIES

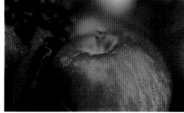

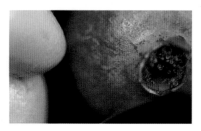

The wealth of fruits and berries available in autumn provides the floral designer with a host of new material to work with, spanning the red and yellow spectrums from deep plum to pale orange.

COTONEASTER RED

POMEGRANATE RED

CRANBERRY RED

CRABAPPLE RED

IVY GREEN

MOSS GREEN

In autumn, fruit trees and bushes provide the flower arranger with rich pickings of colour and texture. Myrtle (*Myrtus communis*), for example, produces plum berries which add depth of colour to designs, as do those of *Berberis darwinii*. For trailing pedestals and table arrangements, I like the deep black berries of the elderberry bush (*Sambucus nigra*). For large Thanksgiving displays or autumn weddings, I turn to rowan berries (*Sorbus acuparia*). Strings of lime-green hops (*Humulus lupulus*) look stunning in autumn decorations, especially garlands, while spiky lime-green kernels of sweet chestnut (*Castanea sativa*) add interest when glued to wreaths. At this time of year, sweet chestnuts are sold on the stem or in punnets through the flower auctions as are green Costa Rican coffee beans, which combine well with seasonal-coloured displays. Many of the orchard fruits such as apples, pears and crabapples are also sold to florists, particularly the small fruits which are unacceptable to supermarkets. To create this display, *Hedera erecta* – an ivy with upright growth – is wrapped around a vase and secured with a rubber band. Small red apples skewered onto wire stems, berries on branches and skimmia foliage are arranged in a hand-tied bunch and lowered into the ivy covered vase.

DETAILS OF THE DISPLAY

30 *Hedera erecta*
20 *Malus* 'Red Sentinel' (Apples)
20 *Rosa canina* (Rosehips)
10 *Skimmia japonica* 'Rubella'

Other flower choices

FLAME RED
Malus 'Red Sentinel' (Crabapple)
Punica granatum (Pomegranate)

DARK GREEN
Hedera colchica 'Dentata' (Ivy)
Ruscus hypophyllum

Silver is a neutral colour that is common to many winter foliages and seedheads. It is not bold or bright so makes an excellent background colour for most flower types.

WINTER SILVERS

SENECIO SILVER

EUCALYPTUS POD GREY

GLOBE THISTLE GREY

SEA LAVENDER GREY

SCABIOUS SEEDHEAD GREEN

MISTLETOE GREEN

BIRCH STEM BROWN

Grey foliage and flowers appear silver when viewed against brilliant white and it is this 'visual trick' that I like to explore in winter displays, where I set bright, clean whites against silver foliage and seedheads. Silver and grey also work well mixed in with bold colours like bright pinks, as well as enhancing pastel tones by amplifying their soft shades. Eucalyptus, convolvulus, senecio, silver proteas and brunia seedheads are all available in winter. The silver-grey foliage of eucalyptus is particularly popular as it has a wonderful aromatic scent. Perhaps the most important winter silver foliage is the balsam fir tree – prized for its symmetrical shape and long-lasting greenery. The Christmas tree has a spicy resinous odour and gives fragrant foliage to decorate the home or use in arrangements and designs. To construct this silver wreath, loosely twist supple stems of contorted willow into a ring shape and bind it in place with heavy gauge reel wire. Wind 7.5cm (3in) stems of eucalyptus foliage around the wreath base and then bind the rest of the plant material into the base using more wire. The wreath will last several weeks but you may have to replace the senecio foliage at a slightly earlier date.

DETAILS OF THE DISPLAY

10 *Brunia albiflora*
20 *Echinops bannaticus* (Globe thistle)
10 *Eucalyptus globulus* (Eucalyptus seedpods)
10 *Eucalyptus gunnii* 'Baby Blue' (Eucalyptus)
10 *Leucadendron linifolium*
10 *Salix matsudana tortuosa* (Contorted willow)
10 *Senecio greyii*

Other flower choices

SILVER
Clematis vitalba (Old man's beard)
Picea pungens 'Glauca' (Blue pine)

BROWN
Corylus avellana contorta (Contorted hazel)
Salix sachalinensis 'Sekka' (Band willow)

Top
Twenty
Colours

The twenty flower and foliage colours photographed on the following pages represent my current favourites from the palette available to the contemporary florist. Unlike painters, flower designers do not have the freedom to mix their own colours. The florist has to rely on nature as well as the flower growers and hybridisers worldwide – who are responsible for breeding new plant varieties – to produce innovative shades of flowers and foliage.

Consumer demand, however, can go some way towards influencing the availability of specific flower colours. For example, white flowers have always been well represented at the flower auctions and markets throughout the seasons because growers know that this classic colour is always in demand for wedding events and other religious ceremonies.

Flower fashion

In interior, gardening and fashion magazines, the deeper berry colours such as plum, burgundy, as well as chocolate-brown and black are currently in vogue. This fashion-led influence has filtered through into the flower colours available and is much in evidence in my top twenty selection. As the coveted new flowers for the garden and the vase, all four colours are personal favourites – each one is very strong when it stands alone and, when contrasted with other colours, these sophisticated shades are dramatic and daring to work with.

But regardless of fashion, the three flower colours I turn to again and again are pink, purple and blue. This is the colour palette with which I feel most at ease, and often I instinctively mix these three colours with a hint of lime green. Although all three colours are a trademark of my work, I never say I have one favourite colour because I strongly believe that no colour exists in isolation – colour changes according to the light and the interaction with other colours when they are placed together.

Colour matching

One of the refreshing challenges of being a floral designer is that you are often given a colour as a starting point for a bouquet or a colour theme for a large event. Often a person will request a favourite flower for their party such as a sunflower which will dictate a bright yellow theme, or a bride will choose a favourite colour as the starting point for her choice of wedding flowers, or a dinner party event will dictate an unusual colour mix to match the food or interior. Perhaps my oddest colour request was when a client sent me a bottle of her favourite nail polish and asked me to match the party flowers to her fingertips! Eccentric though this seemed at the time, it gave me the opportunity to work with a very dark colour that I have rarely worked with since. The choice was very mature and daring, the effect was visually arresting and the end result tremendously appealing – the sign of a seasoned party-giver.

A growth industry

In the last few years the Flower Council of Holland – the bureau which monitors the sales of the flowers at the huge auctions in Holland and which promotes flowers from the Netherlands – has recognised the growing importance of colour as a market force. Over the last two years, The Flower Council has begun to collaborate with style and colour predictors so that the growers are ready to produce quantities of flowers in the fashionable colours of the season. On one level, this is clever marketing and in the short time that this collaboration has operated it has helped to elevate flowers to the status of a fashion item. Personally, I think our choice of flower type and colour should be influenced not by fashion but by our emotional associations with flowers. These preferences pre-date our interest in fashion and outlive our fascination with having the 'right' kind of flower in our home. The one wonderful thing about buying flowers and choosing flowers is that you can stamp you own identity and personality on the bunch you buy and how you choose to display it. It is like art – you know what you like when you see it!

Left Chocolate 'Cosmos' *(Cosmos astrosanguineus)* is a firm favourite, with great old-fashioned charm. Its rich chocolate-brown petals are the texture of velvet but its common name derives from its subtle chocolate fragrance.
Right Here, florists roses have been dyed blue to produce a colour that does not occur naturally. Dyeing flowers is an instant way for dealers to increase colour choice and bring fashionable colours onto the marketplace without having to wait for the growers.

1: AZURE BLUE

Agapanthus
Agapanthus campanulatus 'Blue Giant'
Agapanthus campanulatus 'Intermedia'
Anemone
Anemone coronaria 'Mona Lisa Blue'
Brodiaea
Triteleia 'Corrina'
Chinese aster
Callistephus chinensis 'Matsumuto Dark Blue'
Cornflower
Centaurea cyanus
Centaurea montana
Delphinium
Delphinium belladonna 'Blue Shadow'
Delphinium belladonna 'Volkerfrieden'
Delphinium elatum 'Barim'
Delphinium elatum 'Barbablue'
Delphinium elatum 'Faust'
Gentian
Gentiana triflora
Globe thistle
Echinops ritro 'Veitch Blue'
Grape hyacinth
Muscari armeniacum 'Blue Spike'
Hyacinth
Hyacinthus orientalis 'Blue Jacket'
Hyacinthus orientalis 'Ostara'
Hydrangea
Hydrangea macrophylla 'Blue Bonnet'
Hydrangea macrophylla 'Windermere'
Iris
Iris 'Blue Diamond'
Iris 'Professor Blauw'
Sea holly
Eryngium planum 'Blue Ribbon'
September daisy
Aster ericoides
'Dark Blue Butterfly'
Veronica
Veronica longifolia 'Martje'

Here, the deep azure blue of iris has been chosen as the tonal reference for colour number 1. Although there are relatively few commercially grown deep azure blue flowers, the choice of blues available in the garden throughout spring and summer presents the flowers arranger with a rich source of material. As a rule, blue flowers tend to look best massed together in one-colour displays as seen in nature in bluebell woods. Although regarded as a cool colour, azure blue can be bright and vibrant as well as creating a feeling of calm.

Azure blue flowers are available throughout the year but this intense blue colour really comes into its own in mid-summer when delphiniums are in flower. Often thought of as an old-fashioned garden plant, hybridised varieties of delphinium offer a wide spectrum of blues ranging from sky blue to dark blue, as well as two-tone shades. One of my personal favourite azure blue delphiniums is *Delphinium elatum* 'Faust' which I have used in the featured arrangement. 'Faust' is available from florists as a cut flower and should be bought when the flowers on the lower part of the stem are open. To create this display, I have filled a cobalt-blue ceramic pot with an oversized block of fresh floral foam. The delphiniums are arranged to look as though they are growing naturally in an herbaceous bed. Once the delphiniums are in place, I have added a collar of anthurium leaves around the egde of the ceramic pot to hide the floral foam. Then I teased the flexible stems of the yellow calla lilies into curves and placed them around the base of the delphiniums. This vivid blue and yellow display will last up to one week.

DETAILS OF THE DISPLAY

12 *Anthurium crystallinum*
20-30 *Delphinium elatum* 'Faust'
20-30 *Zantedeschia aethiopica* 'Best Gold'

2: BRIGHT PINK

Bright pink is a positive, happy colour. It is fun and frivolous and one of my all-time favourites. Bright pink flowers are available all year round, but for me it is typically a mid-summer colour.

Bright pink is a saturated hue with purple and red in its colour make-up. In my work, I tend to use bright pinks with deep colours or white but it seems to mix with most flower colours except yellows and peaches. Currently, pink flowers are popular, as all things floral, feminine and pretty are in vogue. Fashionable pink flowers include *Bellis perennis* 'Pomponette' – tiny double daisies grown in Italy, and bright pink peonies, such as *Paeonia* 'Bowl of Beauty', although they only flower for a few weeks in summer. In autumn, amaryllis and nerines are favourites with contemporary florists. To create this round table display, use a 30cm (12in) straight-sided glass bowl and fill it with fresh floral foam. Cover the foam with trails of love-lies-bleeding (*Amaranthus caudatus*). Next, arrange the flowers in tight-knit groups, radiating from the central point to form a dome shape. To finish off the display, skewer fresh strawberries on bamboo sticks and tuck them in amongst the flowers.

Amaryllis
Amaryllis belladonna 'Barberton'
Anthurium
Anthurium 'Maryland Royal'
Astilbe
Astilbe 'Cattleya"
Bergamot
Monarda 'Mahogany'
Bougainvillea
Bougainvillea 'Miss Manilla'
Bouvardia
Bouvardia 'Pink Luck'
Carnation
Dianthus 'Miledy Brilliant'
Dahlia
Dahlia 'Pontiac'
Freesia
Freesia 'Pallas'
Gerbera
Gerbera 'Magnum'
Gerbera 'Rosula'
Lily
Lilium orientale 'Acapulco'
Lilium orientale 'Medusa'
Lilium orientale 'Sorbonne'
Nerine
Nerine bowdenii 'Favoriet'
Peony
Paeonia 'Karl Rosenfield'
Paeonia 'Pink Panther'
Veronica
Veronica spicata 'Ellen'
Rose
Rosa 'Ballet'
Rosa 'Ravel'
Spray carnation
Dianthus 'Curacao'
Spray rose
Rosa 'Christian'
Stock
Matthiola incana 'Lena'
Tulip
Tulipa 'Queen of Marvel'
Tulipa 'Rosario'

DETAILS OF THE DISPLAY

10 *Alchemilla mollis* (Lady's mantle)
10 *Astilbe* 'Bressingham Beauty'
15 *Astrantia major* 'Hadspen Blood'
5 *Hydrangea macrophylla* 'Red Star'
10 *Senecio greyii*
7 *Paeonia* 'Sarah Bernhardt'
7 *Rosa* 'Christian'
15 *Rosa* 'Extase'
12 *Rosa* 'Jacaranda'
20 Strawberries
7 *Zantedeschia aethiopica* 'Dusty Pink'

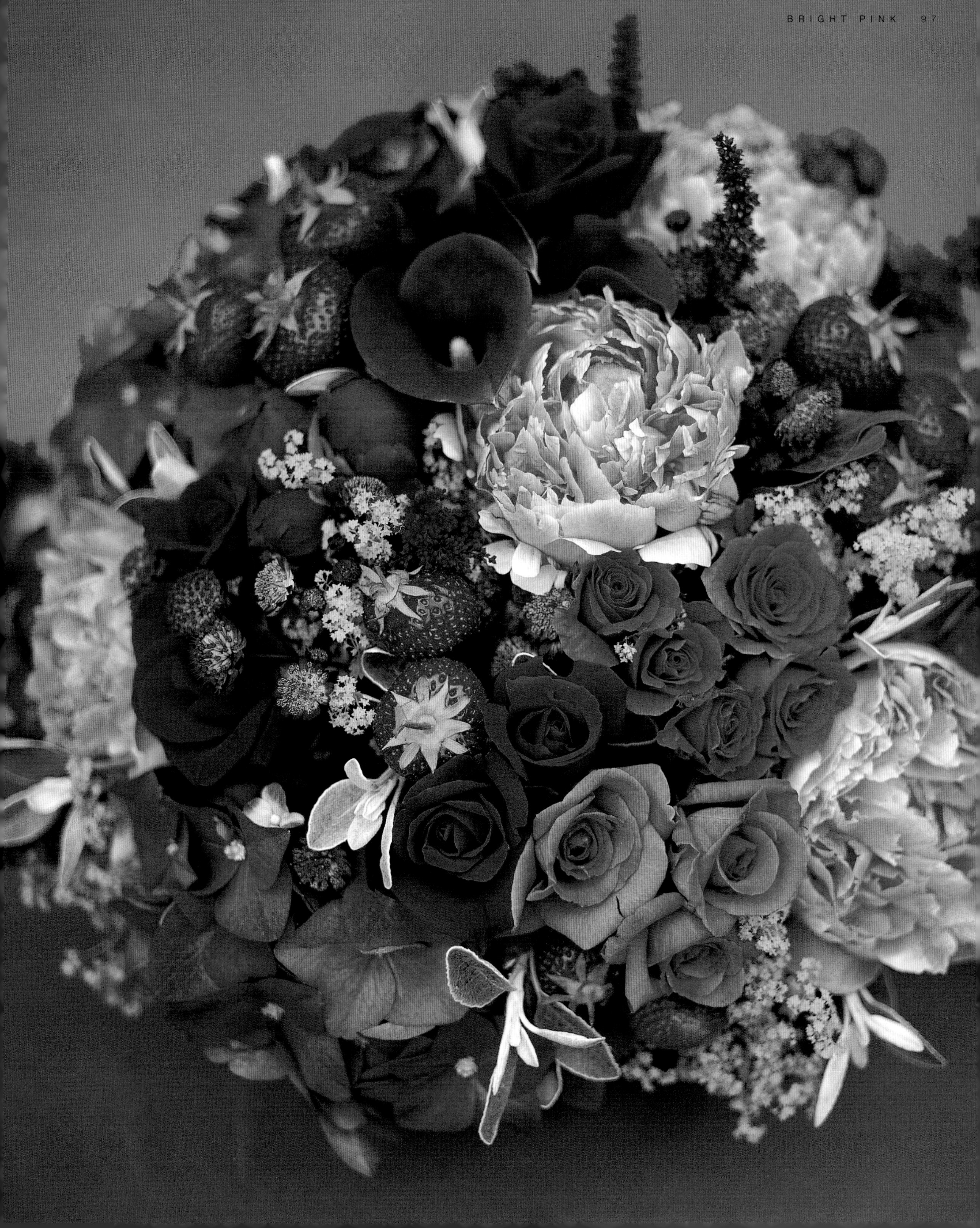

3: LIME GREEN

Anthurium
Anthurium 'Midori'

Asclepias
Asclepias physocarpa 'Moby Dick'

Bells of Ireland
Molucella laevis

Bupleurum
Bupleurum griffithii

Calla lily
Zantedeschia aethiopica 'Green Goddess'

Carnation
Dianthus 'Prado'

Celosia
Celosia argentea 'Bombay Green'

Chrysanthemum
Dendranthema indicum 'Kermit'

Dahlia
Dahlia 'Karma Serena'

Dill
Anethum graveolens

Euphorbia
Euphorbia characias 'Black Pearl'
Euphorbia polychroma

Guelder rose
Viburnum opulus

Hellebore
Helleborus argutifolius
Helleborus orientalis 'Sirius'

Kangaroo paw
Anigozanthos flavidus (green)

Lady's mantle
Alchemilla mollis

Lisianthus
Eustoma 'Fuji Green'

Pineapple flower
Eucomis bicolor

Reseda
Reseda luteola

Rose
Rosa 'Emerald'
Rosa 'Jade'

Spray carnation
Dianthus 'Green Magic'

Tobacco plant
Nicotiana 'Lime Green'
Nicotiana x *sanderae*

Zinnia
Zinnia elegans 'Envy'

Lime green is a high profile colour in flowers and home interiors. Perhaps one of the reasons why it is so popular with contemporary florists is that the zingy acid tone of the flowers freshens and lifts the effect of adjacent flower and foliage colours giving the finished display a palpable energy. In spring, I'm drawn to the subtle lime green of the guelder rose, while in summer I turn to the simple flowers of tobacco plants and frothy clusters of lady's mantle. In autumn, lime-green zinnias and young hydrangea heads do the trick, while all-year round favourites include spray carnations and chrysanthemums. As an alternative to lime-green flower colour, I also turn to fruits, like the crisp lime green offered by Granny Smith apples, and fresh limes.

Lime green has a greater concentration of yellow in its colour compostion than other shades of green. As a result, it does not blend quite so easily with bright yellows unless rich, dark colours like deep red or burgundy, or bright colours, including fuchsia pink or orange are also present. But the addition of plenty of glossy dark green leaves to a display will help to 'quieten' lime-green and create a harmonious relationship with other flower colours. Try to avoid the artificially dyed lime-green flowers which are commonly sold in the US for St. Patrick's Day celebrations. These include dyed green chrysanthemums and Singapore orchids whose stems are dipped in the dye so that the flower is forced to drink the artificial colour.

This single-stem display bows to the current trend in floristry for 'deconstructing the flower arrangement', where simplicity is the key and flowers are placed in surprising circumstances, such as out of water or upside-down in a vase. The two gladioli stems (*Gladiolus* 'Woodpecker') follow the natural line of the vase neck and pick up the fresh lime-green stripe in the handblown glass, while lacy heads of pale lime carnations (*Dianthus* 'Prado') form a protective ground cover for the glass vessels to nestle in.

DETAILS OF THE DISPLAY
20-40 *Dianthus* 'Prado'
2 *Gladiolus* 'Woodpecker'

LATE SUMMER APPLE BASKET

To create this fresh lime green basket, use heavy gauge stub wires to wire up the Granny Smith apples. Then attach the fruits to the outer edge of the sturdy open-weave basket. Place a plastic bowl filled with fresh floral foam inside the basket. Make sure that the floral foam sits at least 2.5cm (1in) higher than the edge of the basket so that you can build up a dome-shaped display. Start by arranging the bulky heads of ornamental cabbage and the sedum flowerheads in the fresh foam. Then place bunches of silver-grey sage leaves and eucalyptus foliage around the edge of the foam. Keep turning the arrangement as you work to create an even display when viewed from any angle. Arrange the flowers among the foliage so that they appear to be radiating out from the centre. In late autumn, you can create a similar display with a red and plum colour theme, using red apples with blackberries, amaranthus, dahlias and zinnias.

DETAILS OF THE DISPLAY

5 *Brassica oleracea* 'Coblanc' (Ornamental cabbage)
10 *Dahlia* 'Karma Serena'
7 *Eucalyptus polyanthemos*
30 Granny Smith apples
8 *Rosa* 'Avalanche'
8 *Rosa* 'Emerald'
7 *Salvia officinalis pupurascens* (Sage)
7 *Sedum telephium* 'Atropurpureum'
12 *Zinnia* 'Envy'

CONTEMPORARY VASE

Kangaroo paw originated in
Australia but is now grown extensively in
the flower-producing regions of the world. It is
valued for its stately textural flowers and leafless
stems which contribute an architectural simplicity
to displays. I prefer to use kangaroo paw on its
own in arrangements so I can fully apppreciate the
elegant stems and tubular flowers.

  For this tall vase display, arrange about 30 stems
of kangaroo paw in fresh floral foam. Place three
layers of West Indian gherkin fruit around the rim
of the vase. Wire the individual gherkin fruit to one
another to prevent them from falling out of the
display. This vase arrangement will last up to three
weeks, depending on the room temperature. The
gherkins do not need any moisture but make sure
that you keep the floral foam topped up with water
to prevent the flowers from wilting prematurely.

DETAILS OF THE DISPLAY

30 *Anigozanthos flavidus* (Kangaroo paw)
30 *Cucumis anguria* (West Indian gherkin)

4: WHITE

Amaryllis
Hippeastrum 'Ludwig Dazzler'
Hippeastrum 'Mont Blanc'
Anemone
Anemone coronaria
'Mona Lisa White'
Anthurium
Anthurium 'Acropolis'
Bouvardia
Bouvardia 'Artemis'
Bouvardia 'Royal Jowhite'
Campanula
Campanula pyramidalis 'Alba'
Chincherinchee
Ornithogalum thyrsoides 'Mount Fuji'
Christmas rose
Helleborus niger
Gerbera
Gerbera 'Bianca'
Gladioli
Gladioli colvillei 'Alba'
Grape hyacinth
Muscari botryoides f. 'Album'
Lilac
Syringa 'Mad Florent Stepman'
Lily
Lilium grandiflorum 'Casablanca'
Lily-of-the-valley
Convallaria majalis
Lisianthus
Eustoma russellianum
'Mariachi White'
Orchid
Phalaenopsis omega
Peony
Paeonia 'Duchesse de Nemours'
Queen Anne's lace
Ammi majus
Rose
Rosa 'Akito'
Snowflake
Ornithogalum montanum
Star-of-Bethlehem
Ornithogalum arabicum
Tulip
Tulipa 'White Dream'

Strictly speaking, white is not a colour but the absence of colour. But for gardeners and flower arrangers alike white flowers are very special and are used as the feature flower on which whole planting schemes or floral designs are based. Many of the most fragrant flowers are white, including jasmine, lily-of-the-valley, stephanotis, tuberose, freesia, and paperwhite narcissus, which perhaps accounts for their enduring popularity. For the flower arranger, white flowers are the mainstay of decorations for our civil and religious celebrations from birth to death. Although white flowers are available worldwide, the majority grow in colder northern climates.

STANDING BOUQUET OF PEACE LILIES

Usually sold as houseplants in pots, peace lilies
are occasionally sold as a cut flower when the
blooms are in bud. To create this free-standing
display, wind the tight-budded stems into a spiral
bunch and bind together the tops of the stems with
50cm (20in) of seagrass rope. Trim the stem ends
to one length so that the display will stand up on
its own when placed on a flat surface. If the flowers
have been well-conditioned, they will last for up to
24 hours out of water. This simple standing
bouquet makes a wonderful table centrepiece for a
special occasion. Other white flowers that will
produce a similar effect – on a smaller scale –
include calla lilies, chincherinchee or snowdrops.

DETAILS OF THE DISPLAY
50 *Spathiphyllum floribundum*
(Peace lily)

SCENTED WHITE FLOWERS AND CANDLES

For entertaining on warm summer evenings, try this simple group of scented white flowers and candles to decorate your dining table. To make the ball-shaped rose display, soak a small ball of fresh floral foam in water and trim the rose stems to 2.5cm (1in) lengths. Cover the entire foam ball in roses and place the ball inside a glass container. Spray-mist the roses with water to keep them fresh. Next, fill a square glass dish with 2.5cm (1in) water and arrange the stephanotis pips. The thin network of intertwined stems will hold the arrangement together. Lastly, place 2.5cm (1in) water in the base of a circular glass dish. Tightly pack small bunches of frothy white gypsophila into the glass container, leaving space in the middle for candles. The roses and stephanotis flowers will last for up to seven days but the gypsophila will last longer.

DETAILS OF THE DISPLAY
25 *Gypsophila* 'Supergyp'
60 *Rosa* 'Bianca'
75 *Stephanotis floribunda* pips

SHOWER BOUQUET

This traditional bridal bouquet has each flowerhead and piece of foliage attached to a length of wire. It takes a professional florist about five hours to make a bouquet using this technique. To save time, florists often work with two or three other people so they can share the wiring and binding. Wiring each flower gives you better control over the finished design. The wire also makes the finished bouquet much lighter than if the flowers and foliage had been left on natural stems. Although these bouquets have always been a classic favourite, they are now back in fashion as the bouquet of choice for the modern bride.

DETAILS OF THE DISPLAY

7 *Danae racemosa*
(Trailing ruscus)
7 *Gardenia augusta* 'Veitchii'
10 *Lilium* 'Eucharist'
20 *Rosa* 'Akito'
7 *Ruscus hypophyllum*
(Hard ruscus)
25 *Stephanotis floribunda* pips
10 *Symphoricarpos albus*
'White Pearl'

5: CREAM

Cream flowers are key to the floral palette. Shades described as ivory, oyster, magnolia, shell and vanilla all sit within this colour band, but specifically cream means white with a hint of yellow. It is soothing and restful on the eye but also elegant. Coco Chanel – the founder of the couture fashion house in Paris – loved flowers in shades of white, cream and ivory and left detailed lists of flowers to display in her Chanel shops worldwide. One of her favourites were beautiful cream gardenias which are one of the most classically elegant flowers for any style of interior.

Achillea
Achillea 'Big Smile'
Alstroemeria
Alstroemeria 'Creme Diamond'
Calla lily
Zantedeschia 'Black-eyed Beauty'
Zantedeschia 'Little Jim'
Daffodil
Narcissus 'Ice Follies'
Delphinium
Delphinium 'Cream Arrow'
Euphorbia
Euphorbia fulgens 'Cream River'
Freesia
Freesia 'Duet'
Gerbera
Gerbera 'Josintha'
Hyacinth
Hyacinthus 'Innocence'
Hydrangea
Hydrangea paniculata 'Kyushu'
Ixia
Ixia 'Spotlight'
Lily
Lilium grandiflorum 'Royal Fantasy'
Lilium orientale 'Georgette'
Magnolia
Magnolia x soulangeana
Ornamental cabbage
Brassica oleracea acephala 'Sunrise'
Ornamental cherry
Prunus x yedoensis
Rose
Rosa 'Cream Prophyta'
Rosa 'Hollywood'
Rosa 'Vanilla'
Snowberry
Symphoricarpos 'White Hedge'
Tanacetum
Tanacetum parthenium 'Snowball'
Trachellium
Trachellium caerulem 'Lake Powell'
Tulip
Tulipa 'Cheers'
Tulipa 'Winterberg'

WEDDING CHAIR BACK

Floral decorations for chair backs have become much more popular with brides choosing a civil ceremony. These floral displays are used to lead the eye down the aisle between chairs. The decoration is a simple diamond shape. The bunch is built up from a base of trailing ivy and dill foliage to establish the shape before the focal flowers – the cream roses – are threaded through the centre of the arrangement in a criss-cross manner. Then stock flowers are added to fill any gaps and spires of lysimachia are woven from the top to the base of the design to add texture and movement. The bouquet is bound to the seat with raffia or just tied to the back of the chair with decorative cord.

DETAILS OF THE DISPLAY

5 *Alchemilla mollis* (Lady's mantle)
5 *Ammi majus* (Queen Anne's lace)
5 *Anethum graveolens* (Dill)
5 *Hedera helix* 'Goldchild'
7 *Lysimachia clethroides* 'Helene'
5 *Matthiola incana* 'Centum Cream' (Stock)
7 *Rosa* 'Alexis'

6: PASTEL PINK

Achillea
Achillea filipendula 'Lilac Beauty'
Amaryliis
Hippeastrum 'Apple Blossom'
Anthurium
Anthurium 'Avo-Lydia'
Astilbe
Astilbe 'Europa'
Astrantia
Astrantia major 'Rosea'
Blossom
Prunus glandulosa 'Albo Plena'
Bouvardia
Bouvardia 'Royal Edith'
Camellia
Camellia 'Spring Festival'
Gerbera
Gerbera 'Amarou'
Hyacinth
Hyacinthus orientalis 'Anna Marie'
Lisianthus
Eustoma russellianum 'Mariachi Pink'
Lily
Lilium aziatische 'Vivaldi'
Lilium orientale 'Le Reve'
Lilium orientale 'Marco Polo'
Nerine
Nerine 'Nikita'
Peony
Paeonia 'Sarah Bernhardt'
Pink
Dianthus 'Opale'
Rose
Rosa 'Candy Bianca'
Rosa 'Vivaldi'
Tea Tree
Leptospermum scoparium
'Gaiety Girl'
Tulip
Tulipa 'Angelique'
Tulipa 'Up Star'

My love affair with pink has endured since the tender age of six which goes some way to explaining why I have featured three shades of pink in my top twenty. The popularity of pale pink as the colour for wedding flowers has never wavered in the US or Japan but in the UK it has been overlooked in favour of stronger colours. Pale pink has made a big comeback and many brides are choosing pale pink peonies, sweet peas and garden roses for their bouquets. I like the ice-cream colour mix of pale pink and vanilla, but avoid mixing pastel pinks with bright yellows.

CANDY PINK DISPLAY

Amaryllis are sold as pot plants but cut flowers are also available to the florist for most of the year. The flowers are graded according to the number of flowerheads on each stem – with the top quality flowers producing four flowers per stem. The peak season for amaryllis is early spring when they are available in many colours including burgundy ('Liberty'), dark red ('Royal Velvet'), bright red ('Red Lion'), deep pink ('Telstar'), salmon pink ('Rilona'), pale pink ('Reve'), white ('Ludwig Dazzler') and a number of two-tone varieties like 'Minerva' (red and white) and 'Apple Blossom' (pink and white), featured here. Amaryllis have heavy, hollow stems and when the flowers are in full bloom they can be top heavy causing the stems to break. To prevent this, insert a garden cane into each hollow stem to provide extra support.

For this display, fill a rectangular glass tank with a block of fresh floral foam leaving 2.5cm (1in) between the foam and the glass tank. Cut pussy willow stems to the height of the tank and place them between the foam and the glass to hide the floral foam. Then arrange the amaryllis in the foam and put the pale pink rose flowerheads around the base of the stems. The display will last for about one week.

DETAILS OF THE DISPLAY
10 *Hippeastrum* 'Apple Blossom' (Amaryllis)
20 *Rosa* 'Bianca Candy'
30 *Salix caprea* 'Silver Glow' (Pussy willow)

7: RUST

At no time of the year are you more aware of the glorious display of colours in nature than in late autumn when shades of rust prevail. Dahlias, zinnias, chrysanthemums and gladioli all grow in blazing shades of rust. These late summer rusts mix well with burgundy, brown, plum and deep reds, while paler shades mix with light yellow sunflowers, achilleas and ornamental peppers. Rust also helps to lift orange flowers and foliage.

Alstroemeria
Alstroemeria 'Tiara'
Banksia
Banksia coccinea
Beech leaves
Fagus sylvatica
Bromeliad
Guzmania 'Tutti-Fruitti'
Calla lily
Zantedeschia aethiopica 'Mango'
Chrysanthemum
Dendranthema 'Biarritz Yellow'
Dendranthema 'Tom Pearce'
Columbine
Aquilegia canadensis 'Nana'
Gerbera
Gerbera germini 'Combat'
Gerbera jamesonii 'Baynard'
Gerbera jamesonii 'Lynx'
Heliconia
Helenium 'Moerheim Beauty'
Helenium champneiana 'Splash'
Hypericum
Hypericum 'Autumn Blaze'
Kangaroo paw
Anigozanthos hybrid 'Bush Sunset'
Leonotis
Leonotis leonurus
Lily
Lilium aziatische 'Monte Negro'
Lipstick tree
Bixa orellana
Oak leaves
Quercus coccinea
Orchid
Arachnis 'Maggie Oei'
Oncidium 'Tang'
Pincushion protea
Leucospermum cordifolium 'Coral'
Reed poker
Cannomois virgata
Rose
Rosa 'Leonardis'
Rosa 'My Lovely'
Sunflower
Helianthus annus 'Fuchsia Mix'
Helianthus annus 'Prado Red'
Tulip
Tulipa 'Allegretto'
Tulipa 'Los Angeles'

COFFEE AND MANGO MIX

In autumn, unripe green coffee beans on their
stems are sent to flower markets worldwide from
Costa Rica. I like to use them in contemporary
displays with the strong architectural flower
stems of calla lilies as shown here. Calla lilies
have become an extremely popular designer
flower. They are available in an astonishing range
of colours from the jet black 'Schwartzwalder' to
the bright yellow 'Best Gold', as well as pink
varieties like 'Chianti' and 'Ruby', and deep
purple 'Purple Haze'. Calla lilies are sold by

stem length, and range from 30cm (12in) up to
1m (3ft). For this display, first arrange the coffee
bean stems around the edge of the cylindrical
glass vase leaving a central space for the flower
stems. Then arrange the calla lilies in the hand
to form a dome-shaped display and tie the
stems together about 10cm (4in) beneath the
flowerheads with several strands of lily grass. Tie
the stems at the bottom as well and place them
in the centre of the vase. Keep the vase topped
up with water and the display should last for up
to two weeks.

DETAILS OF THE DISPLAY

30 *Coffea robusta* stems
5 *Ophiopogon grandis* (Lily grass)
30 *Zantedeschia aethiopica* 'Mango' (Calla lily)

8: PLUM

Allium
Allium atropurpureum

Angels' wings
Caladium hortulanum 'Scarlet Pimpernel'

Astrantia
Astrantia major 'Hadspen Blood'

Berberis
Berberis thunbergii 'Rose Glow'

Calathea
Calathea ornata

Chrysanthemum
Dendranthema 'Payton Dale Red'

Dracaena
Cordyline terminalis

Eupatorium
Eupatorium purpureum

Flag iris
Iris germanica 'Ruby Contrast'

Garden rose
Rosa 'Big Purple'
Rosa 'Deep Secret'

Hellebore
Helleborus torquatus

Love-lies-bleeding
Amaranthus caudatus

Poppy
Papaver orientale 'Patty's Plum'

Rose
Rosa 'Ecstasy'
Rosa 'Nicole'

Slipper orchid
Paphiopedilum harrisianum

Smoke bush
Cotinus coggygria f *purpurea*
'Royal Purple'

Snake's head fritillary
Fritillaria meleagris

Spray carnation
Dianthus 'Tropical Butterfly'

Sweet William
Dianthus barbatus 'Barbarella Light Violet'

Thistle
Cirsium rivulare 'Atropurpureum'

Tulip
Tulipa 'Chinee'

The autumn season offers a wealth of plum-coloured flowers, foliage and berries to the flower arranger. Plum is a sophisticated colour – an intriguing mix of blue, red and black. As a close relation to black, plum is a receding colour that absorbs light. Combining plum-coloured flowers with other different colours can achieve very different effects. To make plum look grand in a formal Victorian manner, mix it with grey foliage. By contrast, acid lime-green foliage makes plums look fresh and modern. Plum is easy on the eye but too much on its own is quite moody – even a touch melancholic. Some of my favourite plum-coloured flowers include late summer dahlias and the garden roses 'Dark Secret' or 'Louis XIV'. There is also a wonderful plum-coloured poppy called 'Double Black'.

PURPLE TIGER ROSE POMANDER

A concentrated mass of flowerheads has become popular for weddings and here, a rose pomander makes the perfect accessory for the young bridesmaid. Garden roses like *Rosa* 'Purple Tiger' are ideal for this type of display because they have fuller flowerheads than florist's roses, which means that fewer are needed. Condition the roses in water for 24 hours before use to lengthen their display life. Begin by soaking the spherical ball of floral foam in water. Then wrap 1.5m (4ft) of purple ribbon around the foam ball and anchor the ribbon in place at the top with wire before bringing the ribbon around the sides of the ball as though you were wrapping up a present. Trim down the rose stems to about 2.5cm (1in) and then wire up each flowerhead. Insert the roses into the floral foam ball, making sure that the flowerheads are packed quite tightly together so that no foam is visible. Spray-mist the pomander with water to keep it fresh for the wedding day.

DETAILS OF THE DISPLAY
60 *Rosa* 'Purple Tiger' (Garden rose)

9: BRIGHT YELLOW

Achillea
Achillea filipendulina
'Coronation Gold'
Alstroemeria
Alstroemeria 'Yellow King'
Bachelor's buttons
Craspedia globosa
Calla lily
Zantedeschia aethiopica
'Florex Gold'
Chrysanthemum
Dendranthema 'Horim'
Cornflower
Centaurea macrocephala
Cymbidium orchid
Cymbidium 'Golden Fleece'
Daffodil
Narcissus 'Golden Ducat'
Euphorbia
Euphorbia fulgens 'Yellow River'
Evening primrose
Oenothera biennis 'Golden Sunlight'
Forsythia
Forsythia x intermedia 'Spectabilis'
Globeflower
Trollius x cultorum 'Orange Princess'
Kangaroo paw
Anigozanthos flavidus 'Gold'
Mimosa
Acacia dealbata
Acacia retinodes
Rose
Rosa 'Aalsmeer Gold'
Rosa 'Papillon'
Safflower
Carthamus tinctorius 'Summer Sun'
Singapore orchid
Oncidium 'Golden Shower'
Snapdragon
Antirrhinum 'West Virginia'
Sunflower
Helianthus annus 'Teddy Bear'
Tansy
Tanacetum parthenium 'Goldball'

Bright yellow is the happiest colour of the spectrum and it is no coincidence that yellow daffodils are the most popular cut flower. Some of my favourite bright yellows include ranunculus, mimosa and forsythia. I prefer to use yellow flowers monochromatically – mixed with other shades of yellow – as its brightness and lightness can dominate other flowers in mixed coloured arrangements. Also, I like to team up yellow flowers that have dark brown centres (like sunflowers) with deep brown foliage and flowers. On the colour wheel, the opposite of yellow is violet and mixing yellow with purple or blue works well.

HERRINGBONE CENTREPIECE

These small chrysanthemums, known as santini, are specially bred so that their flowerheads are of uniform size. The uniformity makes them perfect for large displays where the flowers take a backseat to the pattern and design.
To produce this table centrepiece, a 2m (6ft) long base of fresh floral foam has been been soaked in water until saturated. The foam is then placed on a plastic base so that water does not leak onto the table surface. Mark out and divide up the foam surface into v-shaped areas that act as positional guides for the flowers. Each section is then densely packed with one type and colour of flower. Alternating flower colours are used along the block for maximum effect. Keep the foam moist by topping it up with water and spraying the flowers. The display will last for three weeks in a cool room.

DETAILS OF THE DISPLAY
25 *Dendranthema santini* 'Yoko Ono'
(Lime-green chrysanthemum)
25 *Dendranthema santini*
'Stallion' (White chrysanthemum)
25 *Dendranthema santini* 'Vymini'
(Bright yellow chrysanthemum)

10: LILAC

Ageratum
Ageratum houstonianum 'Blue Horizon'
Ageratum houstonianum 'Escapade'
Allium
Allium schubertii
Aster
Aster novi-belgii 'Blue Moon'
Delphinium
Delphinium elatum 'Barber Pink'
Delphinium elatum 'Delphi's Lilac'
Delphinium elatum 'Lilac Arrow'
Delphinium elatum 'Purple Sky'
Flowering mint
Mentha x piperita 'Purple Sensation'
Hyacinth
Hyacinthus orientalis 'Amethyst'
Hydrangea
Hydrangea macrophylla 'Lilacina'
Iris
Iris 'Mercedes'
Leucocoryne
Leucocoryne purpurea
Lilac
Syringa vulgaris 'Hugo Koster'
Syringa vulgaris 'Sensation'
Lisianthus
Eustoma 'Lilac Fuji'
Platycodon
Platycodon grandiflorus
Rose
Rosa 'Bluebird'
Rosa 'Little Silver'
Rosa 'Mainzer Fastnach'
Sea holly
Eryngium alpinum
Sea lavender
Limonium latifolium 'Tall Emille'
Statice
Limonium sinuatum 'Jolly Birds'
Stock
Matthiola incana 'Lucinda Lavender'
Sweet pea
Lathyrus odoratus 'Lila'
Trachelium
Trachelium caeruleum 'Benary Blauw'

Flowers in shades of lilac mark the beginning of warmer weather and many of them like lilac (Syringa species) itself and hyacinth, have the most glorious perfume. Lilac, from which the flower colour takes its name, is my most cherished flower in this colour group. The cultivated varieties of lilac that are sold as cut flowers usually bear little or no relation to the shrub because they tend to be propagated by grafting and are forced to bloom early in the hothouse. Lilac has been at the top of the list for fashion and interior design for the last few years and this trend has been picked up by flower growers. The biggest growth in lilac shades has been in the Eustoma family with many single and double flowers available.

COLUMN OF FLOWERS

This large display stands about 3m (6ft) tall. Jumbo blocks of fresh floral foam have been pinned together to create a column of foam and trimmed to fit the galvanized zinc planter. The foam is then covered with a frame of chicken wire to hold it in place. The selection of lilac flowers makes a richly scented monochromatic display. Normally, I would use large-headed flowers for a big display like this but lilac flowers tend to be fairly delicate. To counteract this, I have used the flowers in large clusters. A display this size takes a long time to build up – perhaps a whole day – and all the flowers have to be well-conditioned beforehand. Start with the stronger flowerheads like the woody lilac stems and sprigs of brunia and then turn to the tulips, roses, sweet peas and hyacinths. Finally, I have added a few branches of magnolia. This grand arrangement would make a dramatic entrance to a spring wedding party. If you are on a budget, you can use less expensive material such as sea lavender, statice and sea holly to create a similar effect.

DETAILS OF THE DISPLAY

60 *Brunia albiflora* (dyed mauve)
25 *Hyacinthus orientalis* 'Milka'
50 *Lathyrus odoratus* (Sweet pea)
5 *Magnolia liliflora*
'Nigra' branches
60 *Rosa* 'Blue Curiosa'
50 *Syringa vulgaris*
'Hugo Koster' (Lilac)
50 *Tulipa* 'Double Price'

11: BLACK

Rare and desirable, black flowers can demand the highest prices. As a flower colour, black has been highly prized since the tulip mania of the seventeenth century. As in fashion, black is considered chic.

Aeonium
Aeonium arboreum 'Zwartkop'
Black bamboo
Phyllostachys nigra
Blackberry
Rubus lacinatus
Calla lily
Zantedeschia aethiopica
'Schwarzwalder'
Cornflower
Centaurea cyanus
'Black Boy'
Dahlia
Dahlia 'Black Monarch'
Dahlia 'Black Night'
Dahlia 'Black Queen'
Dogwood
Cornus alba 'Kesselringii'
Cornus sericea
Fritillary
Fritillaria camschatcensis
Fritillaria persicum
'Adiyaman'
Gladioli
Gladiolus 'Black Jack'
Hollyhock
Alcea rosea 'Nigra'
Indian flint corn
Zea mays indurata 'Rainbow'
Iris
Iris 'Atropurpurea'
Iris 'Black Widow'
Myrtle berries
Myrtus communis
Privet berries
Ligustrum vulgare
Rose
Rosa 'Barkarole'
Rosa 'Black Baccara'
Rosa 'Black Beauty'
Tulip
Tulipa 'Black Parrot'
Tulipa 'Queen of Night'
Tulipa 'Renaldo'
Viburnum berries
Viburnum tinus
Viola
Viola cornuta 'Molly Sanderson'
Weigela
Weigela florida 'Victoria'

The first black flowers of the year are Iris 'Atropurpurea' and 'Queen of Night' tulips which create beautifully moody displays. Black and white is a classic mix with white flowers making the black appear even blacker. Black petals also look very sophisticated mixed in with silver foliage. Many black flowers have a hint of purple or red in their composition so they work well with deep reds and yellows. Violet, burgundy and black mixes are also successful.

DETAILS OF THE DISPLAY

5 *Banksia ashbeyi* (Short banksia)
7 *Banksia hookerania* (Long banksia)
5 *Clematis vitalba* (Old man's beard)
20 *Rosa* 'Black Grand Prix' (Dyed black)
2 *Viburnum tinus* branches
10 Waxed apples

WINTER BLACKS

This low table arrangement is constructed on a block of fresh floral foam set in a rectangular plastic tray. Begin by arranging the old man's beard and viburnum berries in groups and then wire in the waxed apples. Then add the banksia fruit in groups of two to three and finally introduce the black roses. 'Grand Prix' roses are actually red but here they have been dyed to produce bluish-black flowers. The dyeing process is carried out by specialist dyers who are based at the Dutch auctions. They also dye waxed fruit. Banksia are species native to Australasia but they are now heavily cultivated in South Africa for use in floral arangements. They are popular with florists because they add unusual textural interest to displays.

DETAILS OF THE DISPLAY
40 Cornus alba 'Kesselringii' (Dogwood)
32 Rosa 'Grand Prix'
10 Rosa canina (Rosehips)
3 Viburnum tinus berries

THORNY ROSE RAFT

The inspiration for this simple display is the use of black lacquer in Japan and their art of raffia binding. Begin by binding the dogwood twigs together with raffia to create a square frame around a flat ceramic serving dish. Then cut a piece of fresh floral foam to size and fill in the surface of the foam, working in lines from left to right and then from the front to the back. Work in wide bands, filling in the foam with viburnum berries, then black roses, red rosehips and then viburnum berries again. Using rose stems that are 50cm (20in) long, remove the leaves but keep the thorns to add interest to the stem outline. Arrange the rose stems in three groups to create a naturalistic landscape effect. The display will last well over one week even though the dyed roses are never as fresh due to the extra time taken to carry out the dyeing process.

BLACK 121

DETAILS OF THE DISPLAY (right)
15 *Cordyline fructicosa* 'Negri' leaves
10 *Pennisetum alopecuroides* 'Magic'
20 *Zantedeschia aethiopica* 'Purple Sonali'

Circular base
10 *Ligustrum* berries
10 *Viburnum davidii* berries
10 *Weigela florida* 'Victoria'
10 *Zea mays indurata* 'Rainbow' (Indian flint corn)

LILY AND REED FOUNTAIN

Take the long calla lily stems in your hand and arrange them in a tightly knit group. Place a collar of pennisetum stems around the flowers and tie the bunch with paper raffia about 5cm (2in) from the base of the grassheads. Leave some loose, wispy pieces of grass to give it a natural look. Fasten the base of the long stems with floral tape to hold them together. Then construct a round base from a ring of fresh floral foam. 'Green' up the base by folding over the black cordyline leaves and pinning them in place with wire. Use plenty of leaves around the outer edge to hide the edge of the floral foam. To keep the calla lily stems rigid in the base, create a framework of bamboo canes inserted in between the stems so that they are hidden from view. Fill in the circular base with berries and then, for a finishing touch, insert the Indian flint corn. The display should last up to one week and will make an interesting table centrepiece.

12: ROYAL PURPLE

Allium
Allium giganteum 'Purple Sensation'

Anemone
Anemone coronaria
'Mona Lisa Lavender'

Campanula
Campanula glomerata 'Caroline'

China aster
Callistephus chinensis
Milady Series

Delphinium
Delphinium elatum
'Barba Blue'
Delphinium elatum
'Christel'

Freesia
Freesia 'Vancouver
Bel Air'

Gladioli
Gladiolus
'Violetta'

Globe artichoke
Cynara scolymus

Hyacinth
Hyacinthus orientalis
'Splendid Cornelia'

Iris
Iris 'Blue Magic'

Lavender
Lavandula augustifolia
'Hidcote'

Lisianthus
Eustoma russellianum
'Nagoya Dark Blue'
Eustoma russellianum
'Maria Chi'

Monkshood
Aconitum 'Spark's Variety'

Phlox
Pholx paniculata 'Amethyst'

September daisy
Aster novi-belgii 'Caroline Blue'

Statice
Limonium sinuatum
'Crystal Dark Blue'

Trachelium
Trachelium caeruleum 'Allegro'
Trachelium caeruleum 'Lake Superior'

Vanda
Vanda 'Kasem's Delight'

Once precious as a cloth dye, this intense purple hue was reserved for royalty and the very wealthy, hence its opulent associations. As a flower colour, it produces extravagant and exotic displays especially when teamed with magenta and violet – one of my favourite colour schemes. I am also very fond of the jewel-like colours of anemones, where you see royal purple in combination with bright pink and flame red. In fact, purple is a true friend to the florist, enhancing all the colours in the palette. No wonder it is a key colour in my top twenty.

EXOTIC PURPLES

This rare orchid with its distinctive checkerboard markings originates from the humid tropics of the Himalayas and Thailand, but has been cultivated by orchid enthusiasts since the nineteenth century. But cultivation is very limited and these orchids need to be specially ordered from the flower market. They are sold by the number of heads on the stem which ranges from between five and nine. The flowerheads are quite dense and are hard to mix in with other flowers, so they are well-suited to this two-tiered vase arrangement. Trachellium flowerheads are also quite dense so work well when clustered together. A feather boa is then wrapped around the vase to create an extra layer of contrast.

DETAILS OF THE DISPLAY

20 *Trachellium caerulum* 'Pandora Purple'
5 *Vanda coerula*

MOSSY GARDEN PEDESTAL

This opulent design manages to stay quite informal because the flowers are loosely arranged in a bucket without any floral foam support. The bucket of fresh flowers is then hidden inside the pedestal. The pedestal has been constructed from birch wood and moss held in place with chicken wire mesh. For this floral display, first establish the shape by placing the long-stemmed gladiolis and artichokes on their stems. Then arrange the callicarpa berries and delphiniums through the arrangement, making sure all the stems radiate from the centre. Finally, add the lisianthus flowers and place the ivy so that it spills over the edge of the moss pedestal.

SCENTED TRAY OF FLOWERHEADS

This contained, monochromatic arrangement makes a stunningly simple low table centrepiece. The three flowers are all quite delicate and work well when viewed from above or at close quarters. Begin by cutting a thin layer of floral foam, and place it on the square tray. Mark out the foam into a grid of equal-sized squares and then fill in alternate squares with anemones and violets, reserving the centre square for the hyacinth pips. This display is best for a special occasion as the violets will only last for two to three days.

DETAILS OF THE DISPLAY (left)

15 *Callicarpa bodinieri* 'Profusion' stems
5 *Cynara scolymus* (Globe artichoke)
15 *Delphinium elatum* 'Purple Arrow'
15 *Eustoma russellianum*
'Nagoya Dark Blue' (Lisianthus)
20 *Gladiolus* 'Violetta'
10 *Hedera helix* 'Sagittifolia'

DETAILS OF THE DISPLAY (above)

30 *Anemone coronaria* ''Mona Lisa'
5 *Hyacinthus orientalis* 'Splendid Cornelia'
10 *Viola odorata* bunches

13: ORANGE

Bird of paradise
Strelitzia reginae
Blood lily
Scadoxus multiflorus
Chinese lantern
Physalis alkekengi
Clivia
Clivia miniata
Cockscomb
Celosia cristata 'Persimmon Chief'
Crown imperial
Fritillaria imperialis 'Aureomarginata'
Lachenalia
Lachenalia aloides 'African Beauty'
Lily
Lilium 'Avignon'
Montbretia
Crocosmia 'Emily McKenzie'
Ornamental chilli pepper
Capsicum annuum
Pincushion protea
Leucospermum cordifolium 'Fireball'
Red hot poker
Kniphofia 'Alcazar'
Roses
Rosa 'Lambada'
Rosa 'Naranga'
Safflower
Carthamus tinctorius 'Kinko'
Sandersonia
Sandersonia aurantiaca
Snapdragon
Antirrhinum majus 'Maryland Dark Orange'
Antirrhinum majus 'Potomac Dark Orange'
Tulip
Tulipa 'Ad Rem'
Tulipa 'Princess Irene'

The colour orange is an exhibitionist that demands attention. The hottest colour in the spectrum, it can be an intense and challenging colour to work with, but the results can bring a carnival feel to flower displays. I like to be daring, pairing bright orange with vivid reds and yellows, or rich burgundy and plum contrasts. Orange and purple are a vivacious team, especially with a twist of lime green, as are orange and blue. Surprisingly, orange and blue flower mixes are a feature of traditional 'hot' planting schemes in herbaceous borders – a source of inspiration for many of my cut-flower displays.

BRIGHT ORANGE GLOBE

A 35cm (14in) floral foam ring makes the foundation for this autumnal table arrangement. The flowers are inserted into the foam in bold groups to emphasise the different colours and textures of the plant material. Three groups of cool lime-green guelder rose (*Viburnum opulus*) make the hot colour appear more intense. Inside the glass bowl, arrange a layer of orange aquatic gravel and create a still life of driftwood and Chinese lanterns (*Physalis alkekengi*). A large arrangement such as this is perfect for a round banqueting table, seating up to twelve people, and will last up to one week if the floral foam ring is kept moist.

DETAILS OF THE DISPLAY

Glass bowl
12 *Physalis alkekengi* (Chinese lantern)
2 pieces of driftwood

Circular base
3 *Capsicum annuum* bunches
15 *Celosia cristata* 'Persimmon Chief'
3 *Hydrangea macrophylla*
20 *Rosa* 'Naranga'
3 *Solanum integrifolium* bunches
(Tomato-fruited eggplant)
3 *Viburnum opulus* stems (Guelder rose)

OVERHANGING CANOPY OF LANTERNS

The slender shape of this tall-stemmed lily vase enables you to create an elegant but imposing arrangement while still allowing you an unrestricted view of your fellow guests. Lily vases are particularly well suited to high-ceilinged interiors and look stunning when filled with arched flowering stems. For this display, first fill the vase with two colours of sand, leaving space at the top to insert a glass tumbler so that the flowers can sit in water. The euphorbia and Chinese lanterns are arranged loosely in the hand and then cut and tied to fit into the neck of the lily vase and the glass tumbler within. It is best to wear latex gloves when handling the flowers as euphorbia produces a poisonous white sap which seeps out when the stems are cut. The sap can cause a skin irritation.

DETAILS OF THE DISPLAY
12 *Euphorbia fulgens* 'Sunstream'
12 *Physalis alkekengi* (Chinese lantern)

SKEWERED HALLOWEEN SQUASHES

Using two 45cm (18in) garden canes, thread an equal
number of gourds on to each cane. Secure the two
skewers of gourds on to a flat square dish by binding
them in place with wire. Fill the dish with a small amount
of water. Next, tuck the branches of yellow berries under
the gourds. Arrange them so that they form a decorative
cluster of berries on either side of the display. Cut the
gerbera flowerheads off their stems and arrange them in
a row down the centre of the display. (As they will not be
able to drink water from the shallow dish they may need
to be replaced each day.) This party table centrepiece could
also be created with flowers like summer-flowering pot marigolds
(*Calendula officinalis*) or Icelandic poppies (*Papaver croceum*), or *Rosa* 'Trixx!'
(available all year round). A suitable autumn alternative to the ilex berries would
be *Malus* 'Butterball' (crabapples) which are slightly larger but available in a
similar colour range. Gourds are useful in displays as they are very long
lasting. To preserve them for even longer, cover them with clear yacht varnish.

DETAILS OF THE DISPLAY
24 *Cucurbita pepo* (Gourds)
12 *Gerbera germini* 'Calypso'
10 *Ilex aquifolium* 'Golden
Verboom' (Yellow berries)

14: SKY BLUE

Agapanthus
Agapanthus 'Donau'
Bluebell
Hyacinthoides hispanica 'Excelsior'
Ceanothus
Ceanothus 'Autumnal Blue'
Delphinium
Delphinium belladonna 'Sky Blue'
Delphinium elatum 'Sky-Liner'
Forget-me-not
Myosotis sylvatica
Globe thistle
Echinops bannaticus
Grape hyacinth
Muscari armeniacum 'Blue Dream'
Hyacinth
Hyacinthus orientalis 'Delft Blue'
Hyacinthus orientalis 'Koh-I-Noor'
Hydrangea
Hydrangea macrophylla 'Blue Tit'
Iris
Iris 'Apollo Blue'
Iris 'Ideal'
Love-in-a-mist
Nigella damascena 'Miss Jekyll'
Meconopsis
Meconopsis betonicifolia
Plumbago
Plumbago auriculata
Sage
Salvia patens 'Cambridge Blue'
Scabious
Scabiosa caucasica 'Floral Queen'
Sea holly
Eryngium planum 'Blue Ribbon'
Tweedia
Tweedia caerulea
Water lily
Nymphaea 'Blue Beauty'

Blue is the ultimate cool colour and sky blue is perhaps the coolest of the blues. Sky blue sends a message of calm and serenity and does not fight for attention with other flower colours. For the flower arranger, sky blue comes into its own from early spring to summer when many of the blue-flowering bulbs appear, such as muscari and hyacinths. Later, delicate blue forget-me-nots (Myosotis) become available and look fabulous with pastel coloured primroses, narcissus and tulips. In mid-spring, flag irises appear in some breathtaking blues while commercially grown pale blue irises, such as 'Ideal' or 'Wedgewood' can be ordered from the flower market. In late spring, sky bluebells (Scilla sibirica) work well with the pale green blossom of guelder rose. By the time Chelsea Flower show is under way, there is a huge palette of pale blue delphiniums. 'Sky-Liner' is one of the best known and mixes well with darker blue gentians and agapanthus. By mid-summer you can bring together some really large assemblies in this colour tone using brodea, veronica, and love-in-a-mist, while in autumn, I turn to icy blue hydrangeas and late-season delphiniums.

HAND-TIED BOUQUET

Sky blue and yellow is a combination that you often see in nature, particularly in spring. Here, I have put sky blue and yellow with apricot to create an unusual colour mix. The apricot poppy has a yellow centre and the rose petals have a yellow tinge that work well with vivid yellow calla lilies. To create this hand-tied bunch as a special gift, I started with the delicate poppy flowerheads and worked in the muscari and hyacinths, adding the yellows with bands of blue around them so that blue remains the dominant colour. The daisy-like florist's cineraria is not sold as a cut flower but as a pot plant. I have cut and conditioned it before wiring up the stems and introducing it to the hand-tied bunch.

DETAILS OF THE DISPLAY

5 *Hyacinthus orientalis* 'Delft Blue'
20 *Muscari armeniacum* 'Blue Dream'
5 *Papaver croceum* (Icelandic poppy)
1 *Pericallis* x *hybrida* 'Spring Glory' plant (Florist's cineraria)
5 *Rosa* 'Ambience'
5 *Rosa* 'Yellow Island'
5 *Zantedeschia aethiopica* 'Florex Gold' (Calla lily)

DETAILS OF THE DISPLAY
50 *Helleborus niger* 'Christmas Glory'
100 *Liriope muscari* stems *(Lily grass)*
100 *Muscari armeniacum* 'Blue Dream'

WOVEN SPRING VASE (left)

To make the plaited vase interior, lay out the lily grass stems as a series of verticals and then start weaving through horizontal stems. Staple each woven line in place to keep the grass strands in position. You will need to make two woven pieces – one for the front and one for the back of the vase. This technique is time-consuming but the mat will last for several weeks and can be reused if you simply clean out the vase when the fresh flowers are past their best. To keep the area behind the woven grass free of flower stems, place a crisscross network of sticky tape over the vase neck to prevent the flower stems from dropping down to the bottom of the vase. Next, make up small bunches of muscari and hellebores and feed them through the lattice of sticky tape. Both of these small delicate flowerheads can be bought as cut flowers and work well together – sky blue and white makes a classic colour combination for early spring.

DETAILS OF THE DISPLAY
50 *Myosotis sylvatica* (Forget-me-not)
3 *Prunus laurocerasus* branches

SPRING BRANCHING DISPLAY (above)

Forget-me-nots are a popular old-fashioned flower and are associated with love and remembrance. They are available as cut flowers in the early part of the year because they are grown intensively on the Italian Riviera and exported worldwide. Forget-me-not flowers are very delicate and so do not stand up well to being placed in fresh floral foam. Their diminutive size also means that they tend to get lost when used with other larger flowerheads. For these reasons, I have arranged them very simply in a bowl of water on top of spring-branching foliage. For this display, fill a shallow dish with water and then flex the branching stems so that they bend to create a loose informal wreath shape within the container. Cut the stems of the forget-me-nots to 2.5cm (1in) and arrange them in loose groups on top of the prunus stems. The display will last for three to five days and is ideal as a centrepiece for a spring lunch party. As a summer alternative, you could float individual florets of sky blue delphinium on flexible stems, such as willow or dogwood. Forget-me-nots also work well in posies and they are often requested as a feature of a traditional bridal bouquet.

15: CHOCOLATE BROWN

Anthurium
Anthurium 'Choco'
Anthurium 'Cognac'
Auricula
Primula anisodora
Bulrush
Typha latifolia
Calathea
Calthea lutea
Chocolate cosmos
Cosmos astrosanguineus
Coneflower
Echinacea purpurea
Contorted hazel
Corylus avellana contorta
Contorted willow
Salix matsudana tortuosa
Flag iris
Iris 'Ruby Mine'
Fritillary
Fritillaria michailovskyi
Galax leaves
Galax urceolata
Hypericum
Hypericum 'Dolly Parton'
Montbretia seedheads
Crocosima aurea
Rudbeckia seedheads
Rubdbeckia hirta
Salix
Salix fragils
Slipper orchid
Paphiopedilum villosum
Sunflower
Helianthus annus 'Velvet Queen'
Sweet gale
Myrica gale
Tropical pitcher plant
Nepenthes x coccinea
Virginia reed
Ischyrolepis hystrix

Chocolate brown is a natural shade which adds richness and depth to any colour combination. After green, brown is the most common colour in the landscape, but truly brown flowers are quite rare. In spring, my favourite is the velvety chocolate flower of the auricula plant, closely followed by the majestic flag irises, of which many varieties are brown. In summer, I cherish the unusual chocolate brown sunflower 'Velvet Queen' and Rudbeckia 'Nutmeg'. In late summer come hypericum and chrysanthemums. In fashion terms, chocolate brown is regarded as the new black, and in floristry new varieties of chocolate brown flowers have appeared. Recent additions include chocolate kangaroo paw and spider orchids.

CHOCOLATE REED DISPLAY

Here, I've chosen some rich brown tropical reeds and arranged them with some temperate reeds to produce a sculptural vase arrangement. For this display, I have used a 90cm (36in) glass vase. First trim the reed stems to the height of the vase edge and place them around the edge. Then arrange the decorative maize stems inside the vase and add the irregularly shaped seedpods to give this linear display some movement. Top up the vase with water and it should last for at least two weeks. If decorative maize is not available, you could use bulrushes as an alternative, with contorted willow instead of the chocolate-brown seedpods.

DETAILS OF THE DISPLAY

30 Costus stenophyllus (Lipstick reed)
9 Inga edulis (Seedpods)
30 Zea mays (Maize)

COGNAC AND CHOCOLATE TABLE DISPLAY

This is a long-lasting display as both the waxy anthurium flowers and textured seedpods will last for up to three weeks. Originally from the Columbian rainforests, heart-shaped anthurium flowers look quite unnatural so people are always keen to touch them. This should be avoided because the natural salts in the fingers discolour the flowers, turning them black. Because anthuriums are a tropical flower, they are harvested and wrapped in polythene to keep them warm in transit. On display, they should be kept out of draughts. For a long time anthuriums were only available in a limited colour range, but now more subtle colours are on sale, including champagne, deep pink, coffee and chocolate brown. To create this display, a shallow brown ceramic bowl has been filled with soaked floral foam and the anthuriums have been cut down and placed on either side so that they overlap to produce an interesting organic shape. The mix of flat and textured seedpods rest on top of the floral foam to conceal it.

DETAILS OF THE DISPLAY

7 *Anthurium* 'Cognac'
20 *Entada* species (Seedpods)
12 *Zea mays* (Maize)

NATURAL VELVETS

Often confused with anemones because of their black centres, these flowers have earned their association with chocolate not because of their colour but because they have a distinct chocolate scent. Sadly, they are short-lived as a cut flower and may only last for a few days. The fragility of chocolate cosmos stems together with their very dark colour make them difficult flowers to work with in mixed displays. To anchor chocolate cosmos in floral foam you have to hold the flower close to the stem base and carefully guide them into the foam to ensure that the stems do not break. This can be time consuming and requires patience. I prefer to arrange them with a delicate foliage such as hops, alchemilla or dill, or display them alone in a group or as just one or two single flowerheads in a simple vase on a window ledge. Chocolate cosmos are not widely available as cut flowers and for this reason have a certain cachet amongst the fashion conscious. Cosmos flowers are available in other colours, such as pink, white and red – but they are more commonly known as a late summer garden flower rather than as a cut flower.

DETAILS OF THE DISPLAY

100 *Cosmos astrosanguineus*
1 string of *Humulus lupulus* (Hops)

16: FLAME RED

Achillea
Achillea millefolium 'Summerwine'

Alstroemeria
Alstroemeria 'Tornado'

Amaryllis
Hippeastrum 'Red Lion'

Anthurium
Anthurium andraeanum 'Tropical'

Bergamot
Monarda 'Cambridge Scarlet'

Bottlebrush
Callistemon citrinus 'Splendens'

Bouvardia
Bouvardia 'Royal Katty'

Celosia
Celosia argentea 'Toorts Wijnrood'

Chenopodium
Chenopodium quinoa 'Carina'

Chrysanthemum
Dendranthema 'Klondike'

Euphorbia
Euphorbia fulgens 'Red Surprise'

Freesia
Freesia 'Ricagina Orangina'

Gerbera
Gerbera jamesonii 'Ferrari'
Gerbera germini 'Jaimi'
Gerbera jamesonii 'Ruby Red'
Gerbera germini 'Salsa'

Gladiolus
Gladiolus 'Addi'

Heliconia (Lobster claw)
Heliconia caribaea

Lily
Lilium 'Monte Negro' (Asiatic)

Lobelia
Lobelia cardinalis 'Cherry Ripe'
Lobelia 'Queen Victoria'

Poinsettia
Euphorbia pulcherrima 'Capri Red'

Rose
Rosa 'Grand Prix'
Rosa 'Passion'

Singapore orchid
Dendrobium 'James Storei'

Tulip
Tulipa 'Madison Garden'

Vriesea
Vriesea splendens 'Ella'

Red is the colour of passion. It is showy, sensual and romantic as well as being closely linked to Christmas festivities. True red is a very pure, saturated colour as seen in red tropical flowers like heliconia. Flame reds mix well with all colours except pinks and peaches. I prefer to produce powerful monochromatic schemes or simply mix flame reds with dark green foliage which makes the reds appear more vivid.

SCARLET WRAP (opposite)

Ranunculus are one of my favourite flowers because they have beautiful petalled heads. Once a spring flower, the season for ranunuculus has been extended by popular demand and they are now available from late autumn until mid-spring. The rosehip stems featured in this display are heavily laden with fruit and are sold without leaves which makes them ideal for adding texture and a seasonal feel to arrrangements. I enjoy creating displays in which the flowers and container appear as one and here I have wrapped a cylindrical glass vase in rosehips, tied in place with red rope. I have then arranged the ranunculus inside the vase so that their stems sit at a uniform height above the rosehips, creating a two-tiered display. The ranunculus flowers are packed tightly together and any foliage beneath the water level is removed to prevent it from becoming infected with bacteria which may shorten the flowers' life.

TULIP BASKET

Tulips are now available all year round as growers can now freeze the bulb and trick the plant into flowering. The main season for tulips is from just before Christmas until early summer and there are over 500 different varieties of cut tulip available. Although I like to use tulips in mixed arrangements, they will grow up to 5cm (2in) in water after they have been cut and this causes a rather irregular display when they are mixed with other flower types. The advantage of using only tulips is that when they grow they all grow to the same height. To make this display, place a small glass bowl inside a larger bowl and then wind the stems of dogwood between the bowls. Then place a shallow block of soaked floral foam inside the smaller bowl. Cut the tulip stems to a length of 5cm (2in) and produce a domed effect. Retain the top leaves of the tulips to keep the stems strong.

DETAILS OF THE DISPLAY
10 *Cornus alba elegantissima* stems (Dogwood)
150 *Tulipa* 'Prominence'

CRANBERRY RING

Cranberries are very versatile and perfectly suited to flower arranging because the fruit are actually harvested in water and so last well when submerged. The main growing regions are Vermont and Maine in North America. They are harvested just in time for Thanksgiving. Late in the year, I like to place cranberries in the water of flower displays in glass vases for added colour. For Christmas, I pin them into wreaths and topiary trees. To create this wreath, you will need a 60cm (12in) wire frame. Cover the wire structure in sphagnum moss and bind the moss in place with reel wire. Next, cover the moss in red ribbon – you will need 2-3m (6-9ft) of 5cm- (2in-) wide ribbon. Pin the cranberries to the ribbon using long pearl-headed haberdashery pins. Start from the outer edge and work into the middle, and then work in bands around the ring to achieve a well-rounded wreath shape.

DETAILS OF THE DISPLAY
10 x 250g (½lb) bags *Vaccinium macrocarpon* (Cranberries)

17: APRICOT

Achillea
Achillea 'Salmon Beauty'
Alstroemeria
Alstroemeria 'Victoria'
Calla lily
Zantedeschia aethiopica 'Cameo'
China aster
Callistephus 'Apricot Giant'
Callistephus 'Matsumoto Abrikoos'
Chrysanthemum
Dendranthema 'Salmon Granada'
Euphorbia
Euphorbia fulgens 'Salmonette'
Foxtail lily
Eremurus x *isabellinus* 'Cleopatra'
Garden rose
Rosa 'Southampton'
Gladiolus
Gladiolus 'Peter Piers'
Hibiscus
Hibiscus rosa-sinensis 'California Gold'
Hollyhock
Alcea rosea 'Charter's Double Apricot'
Honeysuckle
Lonicera x *tellmanniana*
Icelandic poppy
Papaver croceum 'Champagne Bubbles'
Iris
Iris germanica 'Edward of Windsor'
Lily
Lilium longiflorum x LA-Hybrids 'Donau'
Lilium longiflorum x LA-Hybrids 'Salmon Classic'
Lilium longiflorum 'San Jose'
Pot marigold
Calendula officinalis 'Apricot Sherbet'
Red hot poker
Kniphofia 'Apricot'
Rose
Rosa 'Aphrodite'
Rosa 'Femma!'
Rosa 'Osiana'
Tulip
Tulipa 'Apricot Beauty'
Tulipa 'Salmon Parrot'

Pale orange or apricot is a pastel colour and, in flower terms, there is a clear division between pale oranges and peaches, and the darker salmon pinks. Although related, the apricot pastels do not sit easily with the duskier salmon pastels. When choosing flowers, what makes this even more confusing is that many apricot-coloured flowers are labelled 'Salmon'. Personally, I find the apricot palette difficult to work with, though apricot and pale cream mixes can be successful. My favourite apricot flower is the Icelandic poppy which is available in spring. I like to display its beautiful papery petals alone.

OLD-FASHIONED ROSE BOWL

In the last few years, natural-looking garden roses have become prized for weddings and summer celebrations. The beauty of garden roses is that they are highly scented and they have a soft, open feel to the petals by contrast with florist's roses, which have been bred to live longer but produce tight-budded flowers with no fragrance. The disadvantage of garden roses is that it can be difficult to obtain perfect blooms for a wedding bouquet because they are grown outdoors, at the mercy of weather and predators. Growers have responded to this problem by interbreeding old-fashioned garden roses with new commercial hybrids. Here, the roses have been displayed in a glass pedestal vase. The best way to anchor this mass of flowers is to create a grid of floral tape across the top of the bowl and insert two or three stems at a time. This should create a natural feel to the display.

DETAILS OF THE DISPLAY

10 *Astrantia major* 'Hadspen Blood'
10 *Rosa* 'Evelyn' (Apricot)
10 *Rosa* 'Golden Celebration' (Deep gold)
10 *Rosa* 'Graham Thomas' (Golden yellow)
10 *Rosa* 'Heritage' (Pale pink)
10 *Rosa* 'Julia' (Dusky pink)
10 *Rosa* 'Margaret Merill' (Cream)
10 *Rosa* 'Mary Rose' (Bright pink)
10 *Rosa* 'Southampton' (Marmalade orange)
10 *Rosa* 'Yellow Button' (Pale yellow)

18: BURGUNDY

This rich and sophisticated colour is de rigeur *among horticulturalists, gardeners and flower arrangers alike. Easier on the eye than its harsher sister red, it enhances most other colours, and it is therefore very useful. Currently, burgundy is so popular among growers that new flowers are appearing each month at auction and flowers like the deep claret gerbera, 'Chateau', are commanding very high prices. Also highly prized are burgundy calla lilies, the showy, wine-coloured dahlia and the proud, long-stemmed 'Royal Velvet' and 'Liberty' amaryllis. It is not just burgundy flowers which are at the height of fashion but dark red foliage too. Cotinus, photina and leucadendron have all had their season extended to add depth of colour to displays through the year and help balance bright flower combinations. Burgundy makes vivid colours look brighter, and also strengthens pastel tones.*

Amaryllis
Hippeastrum 'Royal Velvet'
Begonia
Begonia 'Helen Lewis'
Bloody dock
Rumex sanguineus
Calathea
Calathea sanderiana
Carnation
Dianthus 'Joker'
Dahlia
Dahlia 'Arabian Knight'
Gerbera
Gerbera jamesonii 'Bordeaux'
Gerbera jamesonii 'Chateau'
Gladiolus
Gladiolus 'Black Lash'
Kangaroo paw
Anigozanthus rufus
Leucodendron
Leucodendron 'Safari Sunset'
Lily
Lilium maculatum 'America'
(Asiatic hybrid)
Ornamental grass
Pennisetum setaceum
'Burgundy Giant'
Peony
Paeonia 'Karl Rosenfield'
Photina
Photina x fraseri 'Red Robin'
Pincushion scabious
Scabious atropurpurea
'Ace of Spades'
Rose
Rosa 'Black Magic'
Rosa 'Con Amore'
Rosa 'Hocus Pocus'
Rosa 'Tamango'
Skimmia
Skimmia japonica 'Rubella'
Sweet William
Dianthus barbatus
'Barbarella Diep Rood'
Tulip
Tulipa 'Jan Reus'
Tulipa 'Pallade'

CANDELIT TABLE

In contemporary floristry there has been a move away from mixing five or six different varieties of flowers in one vase to using one flower type per vase. This use of a single flower type creates a very strong block of colour as well as a more structured design. I might use three contrasting colours in separate containers or one monochromatic scheme with different flower types. This is also part of a movement to style the whole look of the table rather than just place a flower arrangement in the centre. To create each cubed display, cut lengths of pussy willow and create a grid at the base of each cube to hold the flower stems in place. You need only to fill each cube with a small quantity of water. Carefully arrange the flower stems in place, working from one side of the cube to the other. For maximum impact, arrange the flowers at least 24 hours before the party so that the flowers have time to open up. For the candle holders, place the nightlights in the centre and arrange senecio leaves silver-side out around the edge of the glass. To finish off, surround the vases with long strands of pussy willow.

DETAILS OF THE DISPLAY
30 *Ranunculus* 'Pauline Violet'
20 *Salix caprea* 'Silver Glow' (Pussy willow)
20 *Senecio greyii*
30 *Tulipa* 'Jan Reus'
30 *Zantedeschia aethiopica* 'Majestic Red'

19: SILVER

Artemisia
Artemisia 'Silver Queen'

Brunia
Brunia albiflora
Brunia laevis
Brunia nodiflora

Echeveria
Echeveria elegans

Edelweiss
Leontopodium alpinum

Eucalyptus
Eucalyptus globulus
Eucalyptus gunnii

Globe thistle
Echinops sphaerocephalus

Honesty
Lunaria annua
Lunaria rediviva

Kochia
Maireana sedifolia

Lamb's ears
Stachys byzantina

Lithops
Lithops schwantesii

Old man's beard
Clematis vitalba

Pussy willow
Salix daphnoides
Salix helvetica

Scabious seedheads
Scabiosa stellata

Sea holly
Eryngium giganteum 'Silver Ghost'

Senecio
Senecio cineraria 'Silver Dust'

Silk-tassel bush
Garrya elliptica 'James Roof'

Silver tree protea
Leucodendron argenteum

Verbascum
Verbascum bombyciferum 'Silver Lining'
Verbascum olympicum

Whitebeam
Sorbus aria 'Lutescens'

Since the year 2000, silver has been a key colour on the fashion and design circuits. I find it is best suited to arrangements that are to be seen in daylight or to well-lit environments so that the silver can really shimmer. It is the tiny hairs on the stems and leaves of grey plants that catch the light and make them appear silver. The hairs develop because most silver-leafed plants have originated in arid climates and these tiny hairs help them preserve water in the heat. Some of my favourite early summer plants have silver-grey foliage, like rosemary, artemisia, sage and helichrysum. Later in the year, I like the contrast of cool silver globe thistles against the hot colours of foxtail lilies, dahlias and red hot pokers. Being lighter in tone than most other foliages and flowers except white, silver complements nearly all colours and can be used in strategic groups to keep clashing colours at arm's length. Silver gives compositions a quieter character and often a more romantic flavour. Using silver with bright pure colours will modify the colours' brightness.

SHIMMERING SILVER TREE

Silver kochia foliage can lend a modern twist to the festive season and provide an attractive alternative to the more traditional dark green and red colour schemes that are so popular at that time of year. It is also a useful foliage to work with at a Christmas wedding if you want to keep the theme light and sparkly – the 'snow queen' effect.

Native to Israel, kochia is available in 60cm (24in) lengths, but in this display it has been cut down to a more manageable length of 45cm (18in). The silver-plated dish is filled with a single block of fresh floral foam. Remove the lower branches from the kochia foliage and insert into the foam. Work your way across the bowl from left to right to create a strong upright structure.

DETAILS OF THE DISPLAY
20 *Maireana sedifolia* (Kochia)

LIVING VASE

Take an elliptical shaped glass vase about 15cm (6in) high, place an elastic band around the 'waist' and start feeding in pussy willow stems. Trim the stems so that they sit just proud of the rim, placing them as straight as possible. When all the stems are in place, secure them with strips of pussy willow bark and cut off the elastic band. Next, arrange the white ranunculus flowers in your hand as a tight-knit posy and feed in the old man's beard around the edge of the flowers to form a fluffy collar. Tie the floral bunch together and place in the centre of vase. Cut the ranunculus stems so that the flowerheads sit just above the neck of the vase. Fill the vase two-thirds full with water. The display should last about one week.

DETAILS OF THE DISPLAY

10 *Clematis vitalba* stems (Old man's beard)
30 *Ranunculus* 'Ranobelle Inra White'
10 *Salix helvetica* branches (Pussy willow)

FLOWERING ROSETTE

Succulents are generally bought as pot plants but they are
occasionally available in flower markets as cut flowers. As well
as silver-leaved varieties they are available in shades of
burgundy and pale green. Here, I have used the flowering
variety which I have cut just above the root and placed in a bed
of eucalyptus pods and succulent rosettes. This shallow square
glass plate display needs very little water and works well as a
low table centrepiece. It will last up to three weeks.

DETAILS OF THE DISPLAY
1 *Echeveria elegans* (Echeveria)
10 *Eucalyptus globulus* (Seedpods)
1 *Sempervivum capablanca* (Pot plant)

20: DEEP PINK

Deep pink is the
most saturated
pink and has quite
a lot of blue in its
colour make-up. It is
the loud cousin of the
pink family. This bold colour is
not to everyone's taste as it can appear harsh and distract from other
colours – it can be difficult to combine even with other strong shades
of pink. It has enjoyed popularity recently as vivid colour schemes have
become fashionable for weddings and parties. To make the most of
this colour, use it with lime green, rich burgundy and saturated royal
purple. Whatever its problems, it is high on my list especially when
I want to make a bold gesture or celebrate!

Achillea
Achillea 'Pascal'
Alstroemeria
Alstroemeria 'Marina'
Amaryllis
Hippeastrum 'Telstar'
Anthurium
Anthurium 'Rapido'
Callicarpa
Callicarpa americana
Carnation
Dianthus 'Charmeur'
Dianthus 'Purple Emperor'
Cockscomb
Celosia argentea 'Bombay Purple'
Corn lily
Ixia 'Mabel'
Dahlia
Dahlia 'Willo's Violet'
Foxglove
Digitalis purpurea
Gerbera
Gerbera jamesonii 'Dark Serena'
Lily
Lilium orientale 'Barbaresco'
Orchid
Dendrobium 'Madame Pompadour'
Phlox
Phlox 'Laura'
Physostegia
Physostegia virginiana 'Vivid'
Rose
Rosa 'Jacaranda'
Rosa 'Purple Cezanne'
Sweet William
Dianthus barbatus 'Barbarella Purpa'
Tulip
Tulipa 'Negrita'

BIRTHDAY CAKE DISPLAY

I often use heather to disguise plastic pots, to make a simple container for a gift arrangement. Sometimes you can buy heather as a cut flower, or as a pot plant from the garden centre. Using a container with a 25cm (10in) diameter, cover the surface with double-sided tape, peeling off the outer layer to form a sticky surface to which the plant material can stick. Then put a heavy duty elastic band around the middle of the container to help you hold the heather sprigs in place as you fasten them to the outside. When the container is covered, carefully remove the elastic band. Then fill the inside with four soaked blocks of floral foam so that it sits above the rim of the container. A large quantity of foam is required because tall candles and a mass of flowerheads need a solid foundation. Insert the selection of rose colours at random to create a dome-shaped display. To finish off, add the tapered candles.

DETAILS OF THE DISPLAY
1 *Erica carnea* 'Vivelli' pot (Heather)
15 *Rosa* 'Anna' (Pale pink)
15 *Rosa* 'Black Magic' (Burgundy)
15 *Rosa* 'Delilah' (Bright pink)
15 *Rosa* 'Milano' (Deep pink)
15 *Rosa* 'Orange Unique' (Orange)

Colour
Charts

I often start off a flower display with a colour theme in mind, so on the following pages I have attempted to classify flowers and foliage according to colour and tone as a design aid to creating inspirational arrangements, and to help you place more precise orders with a florist or wholesaler. Although an appealing idea to the colour-led florist, accurate colour matching is difficult because flower colour can vary wildly within a single species depending on the soil type, the amount of sun and the season of the year in which the flower has been grown. In the following charts, flowers and foliage varieties are listed by name to give a colour reference corresponding to the plant material listed in auction catalogues, available through international wholesale flower markets. In the first chart (*see right*), I have supplied names of roses, tulips and gerberas that tone or match very closely and will work well together in a display. With tulips, the flower names and colours are accurate as they all come from one source – the Netherlands. Roses are more problematic because there is quite a lot of colour variance between the same type of rose grown in South America and those grown in the Netherlands. Gerberas are perhaps the supreme flower for the colourist as there are over one thousand varieties listed in the Dutch auction catalogue to choose from. New colours appear every week – so there should always be a gerbera available that provides the perfect colour match.

Left A single stem of apricot-coloured *Rosa* 'Southampton' is submerged in a storm lantern vase to show off its natural beauty to best advantage.

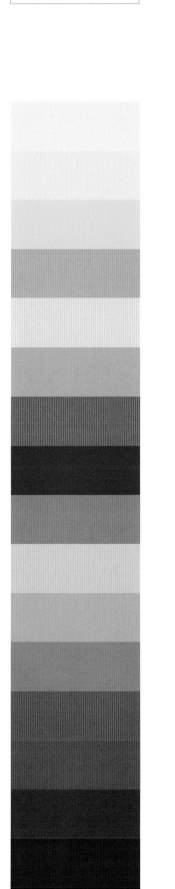

Rosa 'Akito'
Tulipa 'Inzell'
Gerbera jamesonii 'Bianca'

Rosa 'Bianca'
Tulipa 'Casablanca'
Gerbera jamesonii 'Lourdes'

Rosa 'Hollywood'
Tulipa 'Cheers'
Gerbera jamesonii 'Nevada'

Rosa 'Pistache!'
Tulipa 'Winterburg'
Gerbera jamesonii 'Nirvana'

Rosa 'Emerald'
Tulipa 'Super Parrot'
Gerbera jamesonii 'Evergreen'

Rosa 'Taxi'
Tulipa 'Yokohama'
Gerbera jamesonii 'Cosmo'

Rosa 'Papillon'
Tulipa 'Golden Appledoom'
Gerbera jamesonii 'Tamara'

Rosa 'Candy Bianca'
Tulipa 'Angelique'
Gerbera jamesonii 'Dolce Vita'

Rosa 'Charming Unique'
Tulipa 'Rosario'
Gerbera jamesonii 'Grizzly'

Rosa 'Ballet'
Tulipa 'Queen of Marvel'
Gerbera jamesonii 'Shirley'

Rosa 'Milano'
Tulipa 'Marvel'
Gerbera jamesonii 'Eyecatcher'

Rosa 'Mystery'
Tulipa 'Rai'
Gerbera jamesonii 'Blue Eye'

Rosa 'Mystique'
Tulipa 'Apricot Beauty'
Gerbera jamesonii 'Tiramisu'

Rosa 'Catwalk'
Tulipa 'Salmon Parrot'
Gerbera jamesonii 'Zalmora'

Rosa 'Orange Unique'
Tulipa 'Viking'
Gerbera jamesonii 'Fabio'

Rosa 'Naranga'
Tulipa 'Ad Rem'
Gerbera jamesonii 'Mystique'

Rosa 'Estelle de Meilland'
Tulipa 'Abra'
Gerbera jamesonii 'Tina'

Rosa 'Cherry Lady'
Tulipa 'Ile de France'
Gerbera jamesonii 'Estrella'

Rosa 'Black Magic'
Tulipa 'Jan Reus'
Gerbera jamesonii 'Chateau'

Rosa 'Black Baccara'
Tulipa 'Ronaldo'
Gerbera germini 'Black Velvet'

WHITE – IVORY – YELLOW – OCHRE

LIME GREEN – MINT – DARK GREEN

Matthiola incana 'Aida'
Ranunculus 'Ranobelle Inra Wit'

Dianthus 'Prado'
Rosa 'Kilmanjaro'

Gerbera jamesonii 'Dalma'
Trachellium caeruleum 'Lake Powell'

Helleborus argutifolius (seedheads)
Anthurium 'Midori'

Brassica oleracea 'Corgy White'
Rosa 'Avalanche'

Amaranthus cruentus 'Pigmy Viridus'
Molucella laevis

Eustoma russellianum 'Charm Wit'
Tulipa 'Winterburgh'

Dendranthema 'Shamrock'
Viburnum tinus

Anthurium 'Vanilla'
Lilium 'Pompeii'

Phormium tenax 'Variegatum'
Zantedeschia aethiopica 'Green Goddess'

Antirhinum majus 'Pontiac Yellow'
Rosa 'Limonia'

Eucalyptus globulus (buds)
Garrya elliptica

Dendrathema indicum santini 'Yellow Stallion'
Zantedeschia aethiopica 'Cleopatra'

Eucalyptus cinerea (leaf)
Eucalyptus parnifolia

Forsythia intermedia 'Spectabilis'
Mimosa 'Yellow Island'

Hosta 'Blue Moon'
Picea pungens 'Glauca'

Gerbera germini 'Talisa Yellow'
Helianthus annus 'Elite Sun'

Leucadendron discolor
Celosia cristata 'Bombay Green'

Gerbera germini 'Calypso'
Rosa 'Dakar'

Nigella orientalis 'Transformer' (seedheads)
Asparagus retro-fractus

Cyperus papyrus
Papaver somniferum 'Hen and Chicken'
(seedheads)

Hamamelis mollis 'Goldcrest'
Lysimachia vulgaris 'Firecracker'

Anethum graveolens
Celosia cristata 'Bombay Yellow'

Aspidistra elatior
Prunus laurocerasus

LILAC – PURPLE – DEEP PURPLE

PINK – BURGUNDY – BROWN

Delphinium 'Silk Pink Arrow'
Osteospermum 'Volti'

Hyacinthus orientalis 'Splendid'
Syringa 'Ruhm von Horstenstein'

Delphinium elatum 'Yvonne'
Scabiosa atropurpurea

Eustoma russellianum 'Malibu Lilac'
Lathyrus odoratus 'Lilac'

Delphinium 'Christel'
Lilac syringa 'Ludwig'

Eryngium 'Blue Angel'
Iris 'Mercedes'

Leucocoryne 'Caravelle'
Platycodon grandiflorus

Hyacinthus orientalis 'Milka'
Tulipa 'Double Price'

Ageratum 'Escobar'
Phlox 'Amethyst'

Tulipa 'Blue Diamond'
Liatris spicata 'Bluebird'

Anemone coronaria 'Violet'
Tulipa 'Arabian Mystery'

Eustoma russellianum 'Kyoto Purple'
Gladiolus 'Violetta'

Lilium 'Woodriff's Memory'
Rosa 'Anna'

Gerbera 'Pink Elegance'
Rosa 'Royal Renata'

Anthurium 'Spirit Rose'
Zantedeschia aethiopica 'Intrique'

Mini cymbidium orchid 'Alison'
Sedum spectabile

Leucodendron 'Safari Sunset'
Skimmia japonica 'Rubella'

Hippeastrum 'Lilac Favourite'
Matthiola incana 'Francesca'

Astrantia major 'Rosea'
Rosa 'Nicole'

Anthurium 'Rapido'
Chamelaucium uncinatum 'Purple Pride'

Anigozanthus 'Bush Sunset'
Berzelia alopecuroides

Banksia ericafolia
Zea mays indurata

Anthurium 'Choco'
Myrica gale

Paphiopedulum King Arthur cultivars
Quercus palustris

PALE PINK – MID PINK – BRIGHT PINK

GREY – PALE BLUE – DARK BLUE

Hippeastrum 'Apple Blossom'
Tulipa 'Angelique'

Cirsium japonicum 'Pink Beauty'
Lilium 'Vivaldi'

Eustoma russellianum 'Echo Moon Pink'
Prunus species (blossom)

Gerbera jamesonii 'Purple Rain'
Protea cynaroides

Rosa 'Blue Curiosa'
Lathyrus latifolius

Bouvardia 'Royal Rebecca'
Rosa 'Ballet'

Dahlia 'Karma Lagoon'
Musa ornata

Dianthus 'L'armour Lila'
Tulipa 'Grafitti'

Cymbidium 'Miss Pink'
Phalaenopsis schilleriana hybrid

Antirrhinum majus 'Costa Magenta'
Rosa 'Purple Cezanne'

Alstroemeria 'Ibiza'
Gerbera germini 'Sardana'

Limonium latifolium 'Sunglow White'
Senecio cineraria 'Silver Dust'

Acacia baileyana purpurea
Eryngium 'Blue Angel'

Myosotis sylvatica
Tweedia caerula

Delphinium belladonna 'Sky Blue'
Muscari 'Blue Eyes'

Gilia capita
Salvia patens 'Cambridge Blue'

Hyacinthus 'Delft Blue'
Scilla non-scripta

Echinops bannaticus 'Blue Globe'
Eryngium 'Supernova'

Delphinium 'Harlequin'
Triteleia 'Corrina'

Agapanthus 'Intermedia'
Veronica 'Dark Martje'

Delphinium 'Blue Bee'
Gentiana 'Sky'

Muscari latifolium
Viburnum tinus (berries)

PEACH – RUST

Gerbera jamesonii 'Josintha'
Rosa 'Porcelaine'

Gerbera gemini 'Alarda'
Rosa 'Mystique'

Hypericum 'Honey Flower'
Rosa 'Oriental Curiosa'

Rosa 'Pretty Woman'
Paeonia 'Coral Charm'

Lilium 'Salmon Classic'
Chrysanthemum 'Reagan Peach'

Delphinium 'Princess Caroline'
Hippeastrum 'Rilona'

Rosa 'Spicy rose'
Zantedeschia aethiopica 'Treasure'

Dendranthema 'Tiger'
Gerbera germini 'Genesis'

Gerbera jamesonii 'Lynx'
Rosa 'Leonardis'

Fagus species
Hypericum 'Dual Flair'

Dracunculus vulgaris
Salix matsudana tortuosa

CHAMPAGNE – ORANGE – RED

Gerbera jamesonii 'Orca'
Rosa 'Vendelle'

Lilium 'Royal Lane'
Rosa 'Metallina'

Gerbera jamesonii 'Pound Sterling'
Rosa 'Versilla'

Fritillaria 'Crown Imperial'
Gerbera jamesonii 'Amaretto'

Lilium 'Rumba'
Tulipa 'Ballerina'

Celosia cristata 'Persimmon Chief'
Rosa 'Macarena'

Gerbera jamesonii 'Mistique'
Rosa 'Naranga'

Anthurium 'Senator'
Heliconia 'Lobster'

Gerbera germini 'Jaimi'
Tulipa 'Ile de France'

Anthurium 'Tropical'
Rosa 'Passion'

Chrysanthemum 'Klondike'
Rosa 'Amore'

Index *ITALICISED NUMBERS INDICATE PHOTOGRAPHS*

Acknowledgments

I am grateful to Jacqui Small for directing the publication and to David Loftus for photographing my arrangements so beautifully. It has also been a pleasure to work with Robin Rout who is responsible for the wonderful design of this book and Bella Pringle my editor. Thank you to all my friends and colleagues at the New Covent Garden Flower Market, especially to Dennis Edwards for his assistance with sourcing and naming many of the flowers in this book. Thank you too for enlisting the help of your suppliers in Holland, Cees Van Starkenburg and Rinus Renson. Thank you also to Rosebie Morton at The Real Flower Company for supplying the garden roses and for her help in identifying the 'real', non-florist varieties of flowers. Also thanks to the Glasshouse De Sivignon for their beautiful vases. Thank you to Marcel from MHG flowers for allowing me onto your van with my Pantone book and for sharing your expertise with me. Thank you also to Cees and Frank from Ros Flowers, Dennis Bond from Page Monro, Martin from John Ray, Richie from Alagar, Bob and all at Whittingtons, all at David Bacon, all at Prately, and everyone at Best and Something Special.

The Paula Pryke Flower Team have all been very supportive and I am particularly grateful to Ashleigh Hopkins for her smooth running of the company. Noriko Kobayshi has been my assistant throughout and I am grateful for all her diligence and enthusiasm. Thank you to all the others who have played supporting roles; Penny Mallinson, Sarah Jackson, Gina Jay and Samantha Griffiths.

Thank you also to all my family for their love and understanding and particularly to my brother Philip who has been a great support over the last year. Love as always to Peter who graciously continues to share me with my passion for flowers! Finally, a big thank you to Brian Patten for allowing us to feature his poem and for his inspiration.

For more information, visit my website on
www.paula-pryke-flowers.com